RESILIENCE

RESILIENCE

A COLLECTION

Edited by
**Mamle Kabu
Chuma Nwokolo
Nancy Henaku
Edzordzi Agbozo**

The publication of this book has been made possible through the International Relief Fund of the German Federal Foreign Office and the Goethe-Institute and other partners: www.goethe.de/hilfsfonds

© Writers Project of Ghana, 2021

P O Box KD 688, Kanda, Accra
E-mail: info@writersprojectghana.com

Published by **Heritage Lane Press**

ISBN:
978-1-7323519-5-0 Paperback
978-1-7323519-6-7 Electronic

Cover Image: "Resilience" by Amarkine Amarteifio

All rights reserved. No part of this publication may be reproduced, stored in a documents retrieval system or transmitted, in any form by any means, electronic, mechanical, photocopying, recording or otherwise, without the written permission of the publisher.

CONTENTS

Preface 1

Secular Love And What Is At Stake In This Dreadful Storm
   Kwasi Ohene-Ayeh 5

Choking On Hope
   Agana-Nsiire Agana 15

The Old Grey Tree
   Agana-Nsiire Agana 19

I Am Kwame
   Fabiola Amedo 21

How Much For A Soul?
   Hannu Afere 33

Lessons From Essay Lessons
   Aisha Nelson 45

Pithing
   Henneh Kyereh Kwaku 55

Dear Love Or A Short Speech On Resilience
   Henneh Kyereh Kwaku 57

Chi Chi Voices
   Novisi Dzitrie 59

Back To Seeds Again
   Samuel Alesu-Dordzi 77

FAILINGS OF A NATION
  Ikechukwu Nwaogu 83
A WALKER (IN THE CITY)
  Sarpong Kumankoma 95
WAITING FOR MARTHA
  Elizabeth Johnson 97
ESCAPED
  Mariska Araba Taylor-Darko 105
THE LONG-AWAITED ONE
  Priscilla Adipa 113
SELF SEARCH
  Nana Frema Busia 123
BECOMING
  Nana Frema Busia 125
KUBOLOR COUNTRY
  Ekow Manuar 129
FAFANTO
  Akua Serwaa Amankwah 137
COVID-19 AND THE ARTISTIC RESILIENCE
  Wale Okediran 149
COVID DEMOCRACY
  Teddy Totimeh 159
ON UNITY
  Teddy Totimeh 163

ABOUT THE EDITORS 167

PREFACE

I believe that the year 2020 will define the character of the 21st century. The Writers Project of Ghana entered the year with cautious optimism, but as the weeks of this new year wore on, it became clear that the world was heading into uncharted waters. The COVID-19 pandemic, and the task of its political and social management, led to great uncertainty in almost every sphere of life. Across the board and across the globe, major disruptions were occurring, lives and livelihoods were being lost, and there was great trepidation. As an organisation, our programming was suspended, and it was not clear what would happen, for example, to our public reading series, and to *Pa Gya! A Literary Festival in Accra*, which we organise yearly with our partners Goethe-Institut Ghana.

As it turned out, the resilience of the human spirit in the face of adversity shone through the darkness, and, through the timely securing of a grant from the International Relief Fund of the German Federal Foreign Office and with the usual support of Goethe-Institut Ghana, it became possible to organise the fourth edition of the literary festival. This was done in a mixed-mode format, with in-person and online streaming of events. But that is a story to be told in detail elsewhere.

The grant also made it possible for us to put together a collection of writing – which you now have in your hands: a mixed-genre anthology featuring poetry, fiction and non-fiction. The collection was commissioned to coincide with the literary festival and to be delivered after the festival. We chose a rather unique route in preparing it, selecting a number of known writers along with new ones, and bringing them together into sub-groups, each led by an established writer who served a dual mentoring and editorial function. These groups worked together over a period of three months to deliver the final versions of the short stories, poetry, articles, and commentaries that make up this collection.

The mentoring editors and the writers with whom they worked are as follows. Mamle Kabu worked with Fabiola Amedo, Ekow Manuar, Priscilla Adipa and Akua Serwah Amankwah. Chuma Nwokolo worked with Hannu Afere, Ikechukwu Nwaogu, Novisi Dzitrie, Aisha Nelson, and Elizabeth Johnson. Nancy Henaku worked with Mariska Araba Taylor-Darko, Nana Frema Busia, Teddy Totimeh and Wale Okediran. Edzordzi Agbozo worked with Agana-Nsiire Agana, Sarpong Kumankoma, Samuel Alesu-Dordzi, Kwasi Ohene-Ayeh and Henneh Kyereh Kwaku.

I wish to acknowledge and thank the writers for their amazing and diverse contributions. For short stories: Fabiola Amedo with *I am Kwame*, Ekow Manuar with *Kubolor Country*, Priscilla Adipa with *The Long Awaited One*, Akua Serwah Amankwah with *Fafanto*, Novisi Dzitrie with *Chi Chi Voices*, Elizabeth Johnson with *Waiting for Martha*, Samuel Alesu-Dordzi with *Back to Seeds Again*, Mariska Araba Taylor-Darko with *Escaped*, Aisha Nelson with *Lessons from Essay Lessons*, Hannu Afere with *How Much for a Soul?* and finally, Ikechukwu Nwaogu with *Failings of a Nation*.

For poetry: Nana Frema Busia with *Self Search* and *Becoming*, Sarpong Kumankoma with *A Walker (In the City)*, Agana-Nsiire Agana with *Choking on Hope* and *The Old Grey Tree*, Henneh Kyereh Kwaku with *Pithing* and *Dear Love or a Short Speech on Resilience*.

For non-fiction: Teddy Totimeh with the two commentaries *Covid Democracy* and *On Unity*, Wale Okediran with the article *COVID-19 and the Artistic Resilience*, and finally, Kwasi Ohene-Ayeh with *Secular Love and What's at Stake in this Dreadful Storm*.

Of course, I sincerely thank the mentoring editors for their hard work and dedication, which made this project a success.

I end this short preface with the reason we still forge on: hope for the future.

Martin Egblewogbe
Commissioning Editor
Legon, January 2021

Acknowledgements

The Long Awaited One by Priscilla Adipa was first published in "Brittle Paper": https://brittlepaper.com/2016/08/longawaited-priscilla-adipa-african-story/

Chi Chi Voices by Novisi Dzitrie was first published in 2015 in the sixth issue of the now defunct Lawino magazine.

Lessons from Essay Lessons by Aisha Nelson was published in the Phillis Wheatley Chapter annual Chicken Soup publication. http://philliswheatleychapter.blogspot.com/2015/12/chicken-soup.html

SECULAR LOVE AND WHAT IS AT STAKE IN THIS DREADFUL STORM

Kwasi Ohene-Ayeh

"*Color is not a human or a personal reality; it is a political reality. But this is a distinction so extremely hard to make that the West has not been able to make it yet. And at the center of this dreadful storm, this vast confusion, stand the black people of this nation, who must now share the fate of a nation that has never accepted them, to which they were brought in chains.*"

(Baldwin, 1962, n. p.)[i]

"*[B]ut the truth is that no white American is sure he's white.*"

(Baldwin, 1969, n. p.)

"*Still a target
But the badge is the new noose.*

*Yeah,
We all see it,*

---

[i] Baldwin's 1962 book-length essay was first published by the New Yorker as "Letter from a Region in my Mind" and later published as "The Fire Next Time" in 1963.

> But cellphones ain't enough proof
> So we still lose."
>
> (Pusha T., *Sunshine*, feat. Jill Scott, 2015, n. p.)

The phenomenon of general isolation imposed on world populations as a consequence of the COVID-19 pandemic has come with mixed feelings of despair, anxiety, and hope. This moment has also allowed us to witness the shattering of the myth of the centrality of human beings to this planet by the Coronavirus — an undead organism indifferent to its host's age, sexual orientation, class, and/or race. As we entertain ourselves with one social media #challenge after another, we have also, in the same vein, been compelled by grueling footage of unarmed Black people being killed by police officers or fellow (White) countrymen in the United States. The most recent one which has ignited global outrage is the murder of George Floyd by an indignant group of police officers in Minneapolis. The incident occurred in broad daylight. Bystanders could do nothing but only capture the incident on video and helplessly look on. And this comes at a time when the state of Minnesota is hitting its peak in COVID-19 cases[ii], along with reports that healthcare workers lack sufficient personal protective equipment and are getting infected with the virus[iii].

[ii] See article, May 26 update on COVID-19 in MN: 899 deaths; ICU cases hit new high. MPR News Staff. https://www.mprnews.org/story/2020/05/26/latest-on-covid19-in-mn. Accessed on May 28, 2020.

[iii] See Coronavirus In Minnesota: Shortage Of Personal Protective Equipment 'Huge Problem' For Health Care Workers. https://minnesota.cbslocal.com/2020/03/30/coronavirus-in-minnesota-shortage-of-personal-protective-equipment-huge-problem-for-health-care-workers/. Accessed November 25, 2020.

Systemic inequality is in the spotlight once again as minority groups in the U.S. endure the double-edge of trauma (from COVID-19-related deaths) and unmitigated terror from police brutality. As infuriating and demoralizing as this is, these images of modern-day lynchings have become all too familiar in the age of social media. Laughable as it may seem to any creature of mild intelligence from any other planet, we human beings (the ones some swear are the protectors of this planet) discriminate against, disempower, and often genocidally wreck each other based on such arbitrary categories as the colour of one's skin.

Trumpeting Baldwin

James Baldwin's prophetic voice rings timelessly true for our epoch even as he poignantly diagnosed the despotism of racial inequality some decades ago. The latter offers the circular or self-referential logic that there is nothing beyond the stultifying horizons by which our imaginations have been crippled, thereby diminishing the revolutionary potential of love. For Baldwin, love is not merely the convenient reciprocation of what one receives from someone they already agree with or bond with; it is a secular ethic which is joyful, courageous, sensual, tragic, traumatic, and ultimately functions as the cure against seductions of inequality. This is precisely the temperature of freedom, as Baldwin sees it, experienced in some gospel songs, jazz and blues music, for example. Baldwin left the church because he could not find this secular thrust of the Christian ethic in full espousal. According to Baldwin

"When we were told to love everybody, I had thought that that meant everybody. But no. It applied only to those who believed as we did, and it did not apply to white people at all. [...] But what was the purpose of my salvation if it did not permit me to behave with love toward others, no matter how they behaved toward me?" (Baldwin, 1962, n. p.).

Toni Morrison puts it in another way: "Love is or it ain't. Thin love ain't love at all." (Morrison, 1987, p. 194). This fountain of renewal is what constitutes Baldwinian fidelity and the hope of transformation; that is to say where true freedom exists and runs contrary to uniformity and solidarizes for a common cause. Understanding the stupidity and depravity of racial segregation — which essentially posits the self-contradictory ideology of an impure purist system of privilege and disempowerment hinged on the arbitrary category of the pigmentation of one's skin— Baldwin's infinite wisdom and timeless lessons abide. He deploys the secular thrust of love against indignations of racism. Racism is essentially a form of cultural difference based on which human beings hierarchically distribute power — a cowardly and "criminal power, to be feared but not respected, and to be outwitted in any way whatever" (Baldwin, 1962, n. p.). Since existing in this kind of world necessitates differences— ethnic, personal, and so on— one can say that difference in itself is not the problem but the structure of power which any society uses to regulate it. In this sense there can be egalitarian differences, as there can be its opposite. The proliferation of different differences— sexuality, age, race, gender, religion, etc.— renders love all the more meaningful. It means that progress, if there is such a thing, must be achieved through tensions and not necessarily via homogeneity.

Whiteness, like any other inegalitarian worldview, is the practice of taking refuge in a delusion. It joylessly fantasizes about itself as the fixed, provincial, ubiquitous center; it dreams about consensus and practicalizes conformity. Whiteness cannot address itself to the *everybody* Baldwin speaks of in any meaningful way since it necessarily targets and concentrates within the minority for whom its power exclusively proliferates. The pathology that sustains the constitution of white subjectivity perversely augments the paradoxical situation of a desire for a total annihilation of all other races outside of its spectrum (blackness in this case) with the secret knowledge that if it achieved this remote possibility it would also cease to exist. So, it falls on the cruel imperative of subjugation. In other words, it cannot kill them all because in their absence whiteness cannot justify its existence. The relationship is only one of vertical distance, of mutual exclusivity. And this passion for subjection is what corrupts its host; for no person nor group of people on this planet can survive on this bigoted ideal without going mad.[iv]

If we undermine the mutual exclusivity in the above scenario with "communion", which establishes relations based on what Baldwin calls "brotherhood" or what a contemporary

---

[iv] And is this not the hysteria that drove an unprovoked Amy Cooper, a white American woman, to make a distress call to the police after threatening Christian Cooper, a black American man— her fellow "brother" or countryman— that she is "going to tell them there's an African-American man threatening [her] life"?

thinker[v] has referred to as "filial kinship" to create egalitarian distance— the "vanishing mediator" that restores equality in times of crises— it gives us a different picture. Because "[w]hat the Americans do not realize is that a war between brothers, in the same cities, on the same soil is not a *racial* war but a *civil* war" (Baldwin, 1970, n. p.). For Baldwin,

> "[w]hat is really happening [in the U.S] is that brother has murdered brother knowing it was his brother. White men have lynched Negroes knowing them to be their sons. White women have had Negroes burned knowing them to be their lovers. It is not a racial problem. It's a problem [of] whether or not you're willing to look at your life and be responsible for it and then begin to change it" (Baldwin, 1969, n. p.).

Baldwin's indifference to the stultifying fictions of race is telling. He gives us this entanglement between personal responsibility and the universal call. That, in order to fight this cancer of inequality "we have to discover how to reunite ourselves [on] the terms on which we can speak to each other" (Baldwin, 1969, n. p.). But, these "terms" cannot be based on existing identitarian fables, so he cautions that "lest anyone misunderstand me, I'm not really talking about colour, I'm not talking about race, I don't really believe in race. I don't really believe in colour" (Baldwin, 1969, n. p.). What he believes in is the attitude that, at one and the same time, respects the differences we all bring to the proverbial table, which is also

---

[v] I am referring here to the French philosopher Alain Badiou. See Badiou (2003).

willing to transcend those same differences in the practice of emancipatory politics; as in the rallying universal call to action, establishing solidarity, and transcending differences as the way forward. The forcefulness of Baldwin's secular call to love (addressing the *everybody*) in the face of brutal oppression which weaponizes fear is amplified in his statement that

> *"White people in this country [the U.S.] will have quite enough to do in learning how to accept and love themselves and each other, and when they have achieved this—which will not be tomorrow and may very well be never—the Negro problem will no longer exist, for it will no longer be needed"* (Baldwin, 1962, n. p.).

Therefore, one has got to decide for oneself, and if we are to listen to Baldwin's call to subjectivation, that the actual and moral basis on which our world now rests is obsolete and must be changed. "As far as they are obsolete they are wicked, [and] as far as they are obsolete they are oppressive" (Baldwin, 1969, n. p.). And

> *"if this is so, one has no choice but to do all in one's power to change that fate, and at no matter what risk—eviction, imprisonment, torture, death. For the sake of one's children, in order to minimize the bill that they must pay, one must be careful not to take refuge in any delusion—and the value placed on the color of the skin is always and everywhere and forever a delusion"* (Baldwin, 1962, n. p.).

What is at stake in this "dreadful storm" is equality. Equality must be democratic, hence its secularity; it exists for all, and not merely for some. The subject at the center of equality, in this case Black people, exists as a 'vanishing mediator' acting on behalf of themselves on the one hand, and for all of humanity on the other hand (the *everybody*). And since all oppressive regimes thrive on center-periphery politics (where one achieves inclusion only on condition of conformance to what the provincial minority in power determine), all egalitarian counter positions must expand to preserve the 'generic multiplicity' (where one is already part of the social system and can assert independence based on the axiom that 'we are all equal'). Equality, then, is not a crutch, it is already there and has always existed prior to human experience. We do not need to look hard to find it; it is universally available for all who seek, for what we have known for millennia untold is its opposite— liberties contrived by imperialism.

COVID-19 has come with the lesson that the sustenance of humankind is not an isolated question from the health of other life forms, living and nonliving, on the planet. The worst thing is to return to normalcy (and here we thought consuming and being numbed to lynchings on social media is a thing of the old world). If we are to overcome this ideological virus, we all need the "spine" or courage to stand up against injustice. It is not only a matter of Black people in the U.S. protesting these senseless and avoidable killings in the streets, but also that given the contingency of history and power, it could be any of us in that condition. So, plain and simply, rising up for a fellow human in the name of justice is rising up for oneself. Acting on the axiom of equality demands the responsibility of arousing our conscience to be sensitive to one another's plights and never allowing ourselves to be numbed by the inaction of others.

We have already witnessed glimpses of this form of solidarity across economic and cultural lines in our century (the so-called Global Protest Wave of 2019 is a clear example). It has to be insisted on and amplified irrespective of separations in time (histories) and geography. This might seem like an impossibility given the warped and totalistic realities framed for us by empire and capital, but Baldwin reminds us that "in our time, as in every time, the impossible is the least that one can demand" (Baldwin, 1962, n. p.). To speak of impossibility in this sense is only to say that something else is possible outside of what pertains in the status quo; to exult in the redemptive force of justice and true democracy while wresting ourselves from the vindictive passion of unforgiveness. We all carry the artistic duty of creating new possibilities as much for ourselves as for past and future generations. Secular love alloys all these potentialities. This is the impossibility that is already present which must be restored.

Kwasi Ohene-Ayeh is a curator and critic based in Kumasi, Ghana. He is a member of the Exit Frame Collective and blaxTARLINES Kumasi.

Author's note: *This text was written in May 2020, soon after George Floyd's death, and prior to the #blacklivesmatter movement and the global anti-racism responses triggered by this event.*

References

Badiou, A. (2003). Saint Paul: The Foundation of Universalism. Trans. Ray Brassier. Stanford University Press.

Baldwin, J. (1962). Letter from a Region in my Mind. *New Yorker.* https://www.newyorker.com/magazine/1962/11/17/letter-from-a-region-in-my-mind .

Baldwin, J. (1969). Baldwin's Nigger. A documentary film of James Baldwin and Dick Gregory at the West Indian Student Centre in London. Directed and produced by Horace Ové. https://www.youtube.com/watch?v=2zkWshZRm-M .

Baldwin, J. (1970). *An Open Letter to My Sister, Angela Y. Davis.* https://www.nybooks.com/articles/1971/01/07/an-open-letter-to-my-sister-miss-angela-davis/

Morrison, T. (2004). *Beloved. Vintage.* ISBN 1-4000-3341-1.

CHOKING ON HOPE

Agana-Nsiire Agana

'Her breast is full of diverse load,
And she treads a lonely road. No help shall grace her path.
I wish her the strength of her God.

She staggers, limps, drags her woes along,
And faces the blizzards that blow amid the afflicted throng
with whom she dwells.
But she goes. May she go well.
Her home is of a hard place; she was born of a hard birth,
But there's not a heart more tender than the one inside her
breast.
Straight as a bone, she lingers on. Grease to her heels.

But they're covered up in dust; the red dust of her weary way,
The dust of spiteful glances; she's lithe and lay.
Her idea vanishes; her theme disappears, but she's marching.
May the drums beat for her.

A word or two to her lonely ear,
To ring in her haunted heart—she just may hear.
It's good she knows you read her life, you watch and pray.

Her cause is right, and her brow is meek,
Her people knew this and bid her speak.

"Young indeed I am,
And young I mean to stay.
But already as I speak,
My youth has worn away.
You say my load is heavy, but you gave it to me.
My step is slow, but you killed my spirits.
My fingers are frail,
But who froze my blood?

You wonder at my words.
That's your lot; I wander through the woods.
But because you follow me close behind,
Let me open up your mind…"

So, she told him of things both high and low and most secret,
Of pain and skin and bullets and courts
And a forgotten home that still smelled sweet.
She told him of kingdoms greater than his,
And drew their signs into his mind.
And when at length she no longer spoke,
Our blessed King from his dream awoke.

"We must face her every day," he said in the city halls.
"She is challenge, hard work, and reward."
We scratched it on the painted walls.

"She is living for the right to fight and fighting for the hope of life,
She's our conscience, weaknesses, and the undying strength
Of those whose dying is their very fight.˙
We must face her, but first we must find her.
She guides not. Leads not. Only dares.
Dares us to become ourselves."

Our King met her in a dream,
whom I have known six hundred and forty-four long years.'

So a strapping, dying youth once said while caught under a knee,
choking on hope and coughing his story.

THE OLD GREY TREE

Agana-Nsiire Agana

The tree persisted long,
the old grey tree in the backyard, standing among the yellow
of Autumn, dancing in stillness to a song of years
long passed.

It spread itself across the grey sky
spreading its leafless branches long and thin,
reaching for the magpies.

They entered its chilling embrace, adding to the colour of a final smile
before winter wooed it into yet another rest;
A smile for which it grasped the world with its feeblest twigs
and swore once more that it would never die.

Agana-Nsiire Agana is a writer, theologian, and social commentator from Ghana. Agana has been active in Ghana's literary scene since 2004 when he began performing poetry on radio and online. His poems and short stories have been featured in international magazines and literary festivals including Ghana Literary Week. In 2018, he authored *Master the Pidgin, an Elementary Grammar of Ghanaian Pidgin English*. Agana's poetry and short stories draw on an eclectic educational background spanning biology, software, business, and theology—as well as a keen interest in history and philosophy—to explore the themes of identity, personhood, and the quest for meaning in a rapidly changing world. These themes also underlie his current research for a PhD at the University of Edinburgh, where he studies youth digital cultures from philosophical and theological perspectives. Agana has been nominated for a Millennium Excellence Award in English Literature and Poetry. In his spare time, he is an avid birdwatcher and nature photographer.

I AM KWAME

Fabiola Amedo

My beloved people,

I write this letter to you in my capacity as the supreme commander of the armed forces and the rightful head of the Republic of Ghana. Imperialist forces are growing stronger every day, relentless in their goal to topple my government and impose their neo-colonial ideas on our people. It is unfortunate that the armed forces and the police, filled with men who supposedly embody valour and honour, took advantage of my absence while I was on official duty in China to plan a coup against me. They are nothing but cowards, and I, by this letter, order them to return to their posts with immediate effect.

My people, do not be fooled by the benevolence of the imperialists. They pose as nation builders promoting a democratic cause with fake smiles, but they are renegades who secretly will that the united Africa agenda fails! They are power-thirsty and act as though this world is not big enough to accommodate more than one superpower. I have big dreams for Ghana, and the dreams cannot be fully realized until…

"Kwame! Kwame!"

Sekou Touré stops me in the middle of my letter and draws my attention to a commotion outside our shared office.

I leave the letter on the desk and walk towards the dimly lit corridor.

I see a woman standing at the entrance with my closest aide, Dr. Bissew. She is clad in emerald green kaba-and-slit with blue streaks which complement her earth-brown skin. Her navy-blue duku covers portions of her dense, woolly hair which she momentarily adjusts after lifting a toddler from the ground. She seems concerned, engrossed in conversation with the Doc. This woman has been coming here consistently and claims she is my wife. She looks good enough, but she cannot be Fathia, my Egyptian princess.

She looks nothing like her.

I reach for Fathia's picture which I jealously guard in my suit pocket.

I try to tell Sekou to ensure his guards do not let her in. I don't want to see her.

She's always barging into the hallway like she owns Sekou's presidential palace. Each time, she comes with three little people who obviously bear no resemblance to me. She brings food just before lunchtime and I have been suspicious of what the contents may be. I am no fool.

I deduce that she has been sent by conspirators working together with the imperialist forces to poison me and finally put me to rest. Her eyes meet mine and, immediately, she conjures tears and wails, drawing the attention of the guards. This woman must be an actress because she outperforms herself each time.

I dismiss the disruption and proceed with my letter. This letter must reach the Ghanaian press before noon on Friday.

"...until as a people, we resist the rule of oppressors and work to serve our national interests."

Sekou has been anxious all day. He paces up and down the corridor with Dr. Bissew, who is holding a folder with several documents. Their indistinct chatter interrupts my train of thought as they walk towards our office.

All they do is interrupt me. Well, they have good intentions. After all, Sekou was the first African leader who offered solidarity when the news of the coup broke. He offered me Conakry as a second home and gave me a place to lay my head. On top of all that, I share his office with him. I owe him everything.

Sekou and Dr. Bissew are the only people I can trust.

My twenty-two Ministers of State deserted me when the news broke. Every one of them. Some fled to London with the hope of starting new lives. Others returned to Accra, hoping to be accepted by the treacherous coup plotters. If they don't throw them in jail before I do then they must be even more cowardly than I thought.

French is not my forte, but Sekou has shown that language can never be a barrier to our one Africa agenda; not even the foreign ones we were forced to learn from ruthless warlords who demarcated our continent into territories and claimed our land as their own.

We must reclaim.

Dr. Bissew is a polyglot who bails me out when necessary. At least I am able to manage with a merci beaucoup here – to show gratitude, a j'ai faim there – when I am hungry, garnished with nervous laughter and asɛm ben ni. Sekou's response is usually an endearing smile followed by pas d'asɛm. We laugh at the good attempt to mix languages. No problem, indeed!

"Kwame. It is time to go." Dr. Bissew beckons at the entrance of my office.

"Why all these interruptions?" But I calm down when I realize it is time for lunch. I follow him. I go through protocol with Dr. Bissew and Sekou.

Security is tight.

Sekou and Dr. Bissew ensure I am protected at all times. There are two guards at the entrance of our office, six in the hallway and five at the main entrance. It is customary for them to wear camouflage, but I can't help noticing their white shoes and white coats. Perhaps it has to do with Sekou's affinity for the colour white; or it's a symbol of peace. Earlier this week, Dr. Bissew mentioned that Sekou had been engaging various groups to ease tension through dialogue and marches de la paix. I am not surprised. Sekou is a man of peace.

I joke with him through Dr. Bissew that he can never win a fist fight because he is afraid to stain his white shirts. He chuckles but says nothing, probably thinking of a comeback.

We approach the dining area. It is well-lit and the smell of lavender from the neighbouring garden greets us as we take our seats close to the window, on the first floor of his palace. Sekou's love for flora is unmatched by anyone I know.

His colourful arboretum spans the length and breadth of his magnificent palace. There are benches under every tree and his guards are either patrolling the gardens or sitting on benches with invited guests.

A special chef has been hired to cook my favourite – apem with abom. I savour the green and red stew imbued with a unique flavour, testament to the number of days it took to dry and marinate the salt fish in it. I split the apem and begin to narrate how Ma Abena used to prepare it. Sekou and Dr. Bissew smile and nod out of courtesy. They have heard this story a million times, yet I am compelled to tell it whenever apem and abom are on the menu — to honour her memory. We chat about the anti-imperialist movement, mixing Fula, English, French, Nzima and wine.

As I lick my lips to clear the palm oil, I find myself falling. Sekou and Dr. Bissew fade out of view.

Damp ground.
Fresh breeze.
Mango trees.
Ants, in a trail.

I extend my tongue to clean the mango juice sliding down the corners of my mouth. Nyanibah is always telling me how the ants will march onto my face and lay eggs if I don't lick the mango juice. He gets on my nerves sometimes but plucking and squeezing plump mangoes for their juice is one of our favourite things to do.

Mango season is a sign of abundance, and Nyanibah's father's mango trees are decorated with more yellow than green mangoes. If I wasn't his friend, I would have been marched off to the Chief's Palace by now for stealing mangoes from his father's backyard.

I tear off the top part of the mango and squeeze it until the juice appears at the top and slides down the sides.

Nyanibah has already licked the stone in the middle of his mango clean and prepares for another. He reaches for a stick twice his height and swings it at the lowest hanging fruit. He misses. He resorts to climbing the tree. What Nyanibah lacks in height, he makes up for in agility and resourcefulness. He is the spitting image of his father – dark-skinned with tight-textured hair and a loud mouth that always has stories to tell.

"Ackabah! Edziban n'aben!"

My nostrils latch onto the waft of palm oil and koobi from Ma Abena's cooking area as she alerts me that food is ready. I wave at Nyanibah and run home with two mangoes.

I slow down as I approach the shed filled with the aroma of the meal Ma Abena has prepared. I stop to admire how skilfully she cuts the supply of oxygen to the burning wood in the clay stove, flicking sand with quick movements of her hand.

I am reminded of the story of how effortlessly she once rallied men and women in our town to put out a fire. I was told it in the smoke house – where the fishmongers gather to discuss independence, gossip about the chief and his three wives, and of course, smoke their fish – with the usual flair for exaggeration that our people have in their storytelling. Take the one about my birth – "Ei Ackabah, Wo na n'enyiwa yɛ dzin oo! Do you know your mother single-handedly delivered you while walking to the smoke house with firewood on her head?"

This question is usually asked by Nyanibah's father anytime he sees me with Ma Abena, as a way to emphasize the respect I must give her, and to praise her for her strength. Ma Abena just smiles and shakes her head.

"Ackabah, bra bedzidzi eh," she prompts me to eat as she wipes the sweat from her face with a corner of the loosened cloth around her waist.

The thatched roof of the shed is supported by thick bamboo stakes driven into the soil. Poles nailed across the width of the shed form a barrier too small to allow a person through, but big enough to invite a breeze that allows Ma Abena to cool off. She is slender and appears tall when I stand next to her. I tiptoe to increase my height, but she looks at me with her piercing eyes and assures me that I will be taller than her by the time I am ready for my puberty rites in two years.

I grab a stool from the back of the shed and set it in front of the wooden table with my meal.

Ma Abena places a boiled egg on top of the abom in my earthenware bowl and I hand her the mangoes as if to repay her for all she does. She accepts them with a kind but cautious smile. The last gift I surprised her with had worms writhing in it. She fastens her cloth around her waist and inspects the fruits.

"Ei Ackabah, ayɛ ade mmbo; you're getting better at plucking mangoes!"

I smile and place my hands over my eyes.

I scoop some of the green and red stew with my little finger to relish the distinct flavour that koobi adds to the blend of palm oil and taro leaves, before splitting the apem.

Ma Abena doesn't join me to eat. Instead, she busies herself with another clay stove and smoking area which she is preparing so she can smoke her fish and sell from home.

We hear a gunshot, and a flock of birds fly up into the air.

"Ma Abena when can I join Egya Kay, so that I too will learn how to hunt birds?"

"When you are ready Ackabah."

"But Ma Abena, I … "

She furrows her brow and raises her palm, signalling me to be quiet. At first, I think she is trying to silence me about hunting, but she is listening to the gunshots. They sound closer now.

We hear screams, then more gunshots.

Ma Abena orders me to drop my last finger of plantain and we run into the hut.

We hear a violent exchange of words between men at Nyanibah's hut, in the compound next to ours. I cling to Ma Abena, staining her cloth.

We hear more gunshots, yelling and the crackle of fire. She puts her cloth around my nose as thick smoke curls in from our thatch and we are forced to run out. My heart is thumping, and my breath is short.

They are standing outside, waiting for us.

"Woman, where is your husband?" their leader asks.

Ma Abena hesitates, then answers, "He is dead."

"Oh, so you are anyen? A witch who killed her husband so that she can take over his farm and his property!"

"As you can see," – she points to the cooking area – "I am a fishmonger."

One of the soldiers raises his rifle but is stopped by the leader.

"Indeed, a fishmonger who is mobilising women to support Nkrumah! You think we are not aware that your smokehouse is a meeting hub for that?"

"Nkrumah is an illustrious son of the town! Why shouldn't we support him? Who else can we trust?"

I am shaking and coughing but Ma Abena is standing firm and pushing me behind her.

"Woman, you have made a mistake supporting Nkrumah. 1966 is the year of change."

"And you have all made a bigger mistake! I have never seen military men who are such cowards!"

I feel a hard hand on my arm pulling me away from her. I hear slaps and battering.

Ma Abena is screaming.

I am screaming.

I hear a gunshot.

The screaming stops.

They hurl me into a lorry with several other boys bound at the feet while they throw my mother into the burning hut.

Silence.

I feel the lorry moving, but the noise from its engine is muted as I replay Ma Abena's screams in my head. The sudden pain stiffens me. I lock eyes with Nyanibah who is also in the lorry. His blank gaze and streaming eyes tell me that the screams I heard from his house were his mother's. His father had fought with a soldier and paid the ultimate price. His older brother, just starting out as a carpenter's apprentice, is also dead. He is not in the lorry.

We hear the soldiers talk about money they are being paid for all this killing in Nkroful. It's infuriating how they laugh all the time. One soldier is saying that the white man will pay him a thousand dollars and that they want to hit Nkrumah where it hurts. He says he will use the money to relocate abroad with his family.

The lorry finally comes to a halt. We have been in it for several days. The soldiers at the back insult the one driving as he tells them the vehicle has broken down and he does not have the tools to fix it.

We start walking.

We walk on the dirt road from morning till sunset. I am weak, but I have to carry Nyanibah. He cannot walk.

We stop.

The soldier leading the pack says Nyanibah is slowing me down. He hands me a huge stick and asks me to hit Nyanibah or they will kill me the way they killed the weaker boys in the lorry.

I raise the stick over Nyanibah's head and freeze.

My chest is heaving.

Their laughter is like a rusty saw cutting through plywood.

Cold sweat breaks over my face and my knees shake.

I wake up too weak to move. I wipe the sweat off my forehead. I must forget.

The smell of turpentine and paint pierces my nostrils, clearing the drowsiness.

"Doc, how long are we going to be doing this?" A nurse asks in a low tone.

"For as long as we have to. It appears the Aripiprazole is losing its potency."

"The wine-flavoured water worked well with the last dose, Doc. But what if he doesn't recover?"

"Let's keep trying. His wife and children need him."

The doctor writes illegibly on a small chit and sticks his pen back in his white coat pocket.

The nurse collects the chit and places it in a folder labelled: *Yaw Ackabah; Date of admission: 24th February 2005.*

The doctor looks at me, "What is your name?"

"Ah, Dr. Bissew, what kind of question is that? You already know that I am Kwame."

My speech is slurred; I can hardly hear myself. I stumble out of the bed to grab my notepad next to my pile of Kwame Nkrumah books and articles.

The doctor rushes to my aid, but I refuse his assistance. I regain my balance and run for the corridor.

"You can't run forever, Ackabah!"

I plunge, too late, to avoid a scaffold and the painter mounted on it.

I stop to watch red paint mix with soil from a broken flower pot – the way Nyanibah's blood mixed with the sand on the dirt road.

Fabiola Amedo enjoys the art of describing people, places and experiences through revelation in her stories. She is a lifelong learner and is deeply intrigued by the subtlety of the human experience which she brings to bear in her fictional stories and poems; ranging from historical, contemporary to fantasy-based genres. Her passion for reading and writing began at an early age, when she would spend most of her time reading story books including the blurbs and authors' biographies at the back of the books.

She currently works as an IT Consultant at KPMG, a big four firm, and enjoys volunteering. She has also written articles titled, "Interesting Times Ahead: Why Young Professionals Should Consider Careers in Information Security" and "The Rise of Digital Immigrants: Beyond A Pandemic" which have been published on the ISACA website and the Business & Financial Times (B&FT) respectively.

Fabiola's greatest fear is unfulfilled potential. She believes that passion births purpose and is embracing the opportunity to contribute to boosting the local literary scene. She looks forward to increasing the representation of Ghanaian stories told through the eyes of Ghanaian children, men and women.

HOW MUCH FOR A SOUL?

Hannu Afere

Of all the demons loved by God, Esu is the one I hate the most.

This was the foremost thought in Ojiji's head as he steered his Camry out of the parking lot and gunned it down the street.

The second most important thought in his head was how he was going to retrieve a certain package for Di Nobor, his new dealer.

He rolled the words around on his tongue again. *Demons loved by God…*

Had he seen it in a book, or heard it in a song? He did not know where the thought came from, but it seemed deliciously poetic, even if it was borderline blasphemous.

For the first time, three months ago, he had been personally involved in the deliverance of a possessed girl.

Possessed by Esu, the lead pastor had said.

His hands were shaking, just remembering: the girl had bitten him, and he'd had to get a tetanus shot afterwards.

Deliverance sessions required a certain degree of intensity, so of course, force had been used – maybe excessively even.

Of course, any excess was not deliberate for she was a frail host: she was rail thin, with maniacal manifestations.

The lead pastor had ordered them to hold her, but because they were all so sweaty from the strenuous prayers, she had slipped away and tried to make a run for it.

It had been up to Ojiji to trip her up as she ran past him. She fell flat on her face and the exorcism was restarted.

Right now, his hands were gripping the wheel tighter than was necessary. He was still haunted by her expression. Perhaps she had thought him the path of least resistance. Perhaps she had seen some hope, some kindness in his eyes.

He had managed to convince himself that the deliverance was for her own good, that whatever beatings she received was all the devil's fault, was all Esu's fault.

For now, he decided, it would be better if he could just focus on getting the package for Mr. Di.

But he couldn't. His head throbbed. He hadn't had any Ambrosia in 72 hours. His central nervous system was beginning to take a hit.

Outside, the night streets looked as deserted as Lagos in Yuletide – eerily sane – and he didn't know what to make of it.

He swung the Camry around the next corner and came face-to-face with the sprawling architectural miracle that was the Holy Kinfolk of God Cathedral.

It was all sandstone and glass circled by the lagoon. A tribute to the Gothic Revival style from the 1900s.

The exterior was mostly in its original state, neat and imposing, featuring a square tower, pinnacle spire, a slate roof and dressed stonework. The mission house located next to the church was a two-story building composed predominantly of stuccoed brick and a garden speaking volumes about the G.O.'s horticultural tastes.

Ojiji's plan was a simple one and there was no doubt in his mind that he was going to pull it off.

He took out his phone and pretended to be making a phone call. There were five guards on duty.

Walking briskly past the first and second, he barely offered any greeting. When he got to the third, he flashed an embarrassed smile and that one waved him through. He was the General Overseer's son after all. Why would anyone suspect him of ulterior motives?

The fourth and fifth guards were watching football highlights on an iPhone. They snapped to attention when they saw him, but he pretended not to notice. *"Please put Sister Mary on the line, let me pray for her..."*

He walked the length of the corridor and made a left towards the administrative center. There were cameras everywhere. His father's office had an Eye Scan security system. Only family members, senior pastors and the secretary had their retina patterns programmed in. He punched the button and put his eye to the small opening, staring into the amber light until he heard the small beep.

As the lock clicked and the light on the keypad went from red to green, Ojiji could feel the blood pulsing in his temples. He took a deep breath and slipped inside.

He couldn't believe he was actually doing this: letting Mr. Di blackmail him like this. If word got out, it would be disastrous. He would be excommunicated. It would break his father's heart. It would break the hearts of all those who saw him at every service as a role model.

His hand found the light switch without incident and he surveyed his surroundings.

The office looked like it had already been trashed. The swivel chairs were facing the wrong way, there were filing cabinets with drawers hanging open and biscuits and paperwork were scattered all over the desk. Ojiji had a lot of questions. He had never known his father to be untidy. What happened here? Why had his father left in a hurry – if it was him? Where was his secretary?

But the clock was ticking.

And Mr. Di was waiting.

Ojiji was desperate for some Ambrosia. He knew Di was exploiting his addiction to set him up. He knew. He was an intelligent man. But there was nothing he could do about it.

"I gatz find this package," he muttered to himself.

The scattered office could mean any of a lot of bad things. Ojiji did not want to think about them. He couldn't shake off the feeling, however, that there were cameras watching.

He knew how surveillance didn't have to be done by unwieldy, obvious cams these days. There could be wireless micro devices, some as small as a pencil eraser hidden in obscure places like wall clocks, portraits or air conditioner vents. They could take the shape of an air freshener, an umbrella or even a button.

Just to be sure, he could turn off the lights to look around using the front-facing camera on his phone. He knew how to detect the invisible infrared light that spy cameras emitted, but he didn't have time for that.

Ojiji slapped the side of his head as if to arrange his thoughts, pushed a chair gently to the side and looked around the room again.

The safe!

He hurried over to the back of the room, past the cabinets and the wastepaper basket lying on its side. Beside a tray with coffee-stained documents and a cup filled with pens stood the inconspicuous safe. Ojiji paused. He knew his father used a four-digit code, which meant ten thousand different permutations.

He could try guessing, but time was a luxury just then. To narrow the odds, Ojiji ground a biscuit under his heel and blew some of its fine powder gently across the keypad. That was how they did it in the spy movies. He could see now that a tracing of dust had stuck to four of the keys. The one, the four, the nine and the two.

His birthday.

Ojiji was touched, but there was no time for sentimentality. He opened the safe and saw Di's package, its heart shape apparent, even inside the large brown envelope with Sade Adu's face on it.

Ojiji shook his head. Mr. Di had an impossible sense of humor. When he'd asked him what the package was, the man laughed and told him it was his soul, said Ojiji would know it when he saw it. Well, Sade Adu was a *soul* musician, wasn't she?

The package felt soft, yet it was quite heavy. What was his father doing with something like this?

Ojiji grabbed it and immediately began to plan his exit. There was no way he could take something this large out without the cameras picking it up. The alarms would go off. No way he could beat the guards twice. The window in the room was big enough and could only be opened from inside. It took him only a couple of minutes to slide out, drop gently onto the grass and take out his phone again.

The moon was out so he could see clearly. He would leave the Camry on the other side, for now. The dealer was supposed to meet him down the street. He prayed to God Mr. Di kept his word. The blackmail was a good enough motivation for him, but the promise of Ambrosia made his side of the bargain more compelling. Walking was cumbersome because of the weight of the envelope and he limped along while dialing the number.

The face of the girl breached his mind again. The words from the deliverance session echoed in his head.

Of all the demons loved by God, Esu is the one I hate most.

"The number you have dialed is not reachable at the moment—"

Ojiji cut the call impatiently and redialed.

The trees and lampposts cast shadows from across the street. He began to sense that he was being followed. He turned around sharply and saw him.

Once the man knew that Ojiji had noticed him, he looked like he was reconsidering his erstwhile plans and started to walk away. Ojiji yelled for him to stop. Surprisingly, he did.

Ojiji sized him up. He was a short man. Maybe 5'2, 5'3. Typical corporate type, wearing a black herringbone single-breasted suit primed with all the accessories one would expect to see on an executive: cufflinks, tie-pin, lapel pins, blood-red pocket handkerchief, N20,000 wristwatch, Cordovan wingtip shoes, Italian silk tie… not to mention his God-given chocolatey brown eyes.

His afro was thick and properly trimmed. Ojiji knew whose signature that was.

"You're looking for me." It wasn't a question.

"Why would you say that?" the man asked, rubbing his neck casually. He seemed genuinely surprised that Ojiji was talking to him.

"He finally found out, didn't he?" Ojiji's tone was hard.

Mr. Red-and-Black stopped rubbing his neck. "What?"

Ojiji eyed him. His anger was growing. "Look, I know what I'm doing is wrong, but I am really tired of being spied on. He has no right to be telling me what to do and what not to do! Let's just get the formalities out of the way. Are you going to try and arrest me or what?"

"Arrest? Oh, no no no," he said, putting up his hands in a defensive posture Ojiji had never seen before. "I just need to check something."

He looked genuinely confused, but Ojiji was no longer listening. If this man was here to take him in, he would fight his way out of it. He would not let anyone ruin his deal with Mr. Di.

"Eat this."

Ojiji threw a quick front kick and felt himself pushed off balance; he caught his footing and turned. The man looked like he knew what he was doing, but Ojiji had a lot more in his repertoire than a simple front kick. The heavy envelope restricted his movement so he placed it by the kerb and walked up to him, keeping his arms at his sides like he was not going to take a shot. He could see Mr. Red-and-Black's confusion and that let him snake in a quick jab.

The man deflected it and Ojiji growled, "So father found someone who can at least give me a warm up."

"Father who?" he looked amused. "I didn't even know you were Catholic."

Ojiji lunged, bringing three quick shots to his body but the man backed up, blocking the shots before maneuvering again to the side.

"Look," the man smiled, showing a perfect dentition. "I'm not here to fight. All I need is that package."

Ojiji glanced back at Di's envelope. "Why?"

"Because if your friend should get it," he spat the word 'friend' like it was bitter kola. "You'd be doomed forever."

"And why do you want it?" Ojiji asked.

"Because I love you!" He sounded pained, "I don't want you to die!"

Ojiji looked at him like he was crazy. "You love me?"

"Yes."

Ojiji shook his head in disgust. "Get out."

Red-and-Black did not move.

"I said: Get. Out. Now."

"No. I will stop you," the guy said. His tone was half-pleading, half-commanding. "Don't kill yourself. Give me the package, please. Would you believe me if I told you what was inside..."

Ojiji threw a punch at his nose. The man dodged. Why wasn't he returning the attack?

"It's the Ambrosia, isn't it?"

"So?" Ojiji growled, "How e take concern you?"

"What else did he promise you? That he was going to make your case with the girl go away?"

Ojiji's senses went static for a moment. No one else was supposed to know about the girl.

"You got her pregnant, didn't you?"

Damn you, Di! Damn you, to hell.

"You, the son of the General Overseer. You, the natural leader of the next generation. He has the video."

Ojiji clenched his fists.

"He promised you he'd make it go away? Well, newsflash – he won't. Imagine what would happen when word reaches your father. Imagine what would happen when he finds out you have been an Ambrosia abuser too, a common drug addict… for how long now?"

It took Ojiji a minute to plan his movements: he got up close and as soon as he felt the man's hands deflect a jab, he ducked down and planted his shoulder in his gut, then he lifted him up twisting his hips and slamming him down in the dirt. He got into a top mount and could see a bad ground defense as he started to bring a fist down to his face.

It was the familiar yelling of Mr. Di that stopped him. Ojiji jumped off his stalker and retrieved his package. He glanced around for his dealer who was jogging down alone, his black SUV parked just beyond him. The fat around his jowls and midsection bounced as he moved. He looked harried.

"Guy," he said simply, when he came close enough. "Wia my package?" Ojiji held it in front of him. He saw it and rushed forward.

Ojiji chuckled, snatched it away from his grasp at the last minute and wagged a finger. 'Not so fast.'

He pushed his hands into his pockets coolly, as if to say, 'I respect that', then he nodded at Mr. Red-and-Black who was struggling to his feet, dusting at his clothes. "Who is your new friend?"

The man grunted, "Esu."

Ojiji blinked and then he shrugged, "He's not my friend. Creep was following me around like a fly. You saved him from a beating."

"Don't give it to him," Esu said, through clenched teeth. "I beg you. Don't give it to him."

"Yeah," said Ojiji, "he's been going on and on about the package, I said…"

But Di did not let him finish. Whipping his chubby arms up, he shouted "Did you open it? Did you see what was inside?"

"Relax," Ojiji chuckled. "Of course I didn't. Have you taken care of the girl?"

"Yes, I have."

"What does that mean?"

"Means I was with her in the hospital, fool."

"Evidence?"

Di rolled his eyes and produced a tab. On the screen a young lady was being wheeled into a hospital room. It was the girl from the deliverance session. "D and C, post treatment, counseling, the whole caboodle. Paid for. See Receipt. Now, where is my stuff?"

Ojiji could barely look at the video. He was filled with shame, guilt and regret but this did not interfere with his bargaining. He held out his hand. "My stuff, first."

Di pulled out a black nylon bag from a jeans pocket. Ojiji opened it. Six packets of Ambrosia. Better than Ice or Ecstasy. Enough to make him forget. Enough to keep him functioning.

He handed over the Sade Adu envelope in exchange.

Esu let out a strangled cry, like he was being physically assaulted.

Mr. Di smiled. Just then, the sound of breaking glass reached their ears. The front door of the cathedral burst open and from where they stood, they heard the roar of the guards.

The next thing they knew, sirens and police car turret lights flooded the area.

Ojiji looked up, his heart pounding with fear.

Gunshots rang out. Di screamed for him to run, but Ojiji didn't need the warning. He pushed Esu aside and tore down the street. As Ojiji rounded the corner, the fat man turned to Esu and laughed. He waved the envelope in his face.

His own face began to transform in the moonlight.

The whites in his eyes disappeared. His eyeballs became twin bottomless pits. They looked soul-less. Vacant. The skin around his face tightened – became a sickly green color with fat veins. He smiled, exposing filed teeth.

When he leaned closer, his breath reeked of gunpowder and death.

Esu had no illusions what that meant. He shut his eyes.

"There is nothing you can do for the boy now," Di cackled. "He gave me his soul, personally."

Amidst the sirens and blue-red lights, the guards roared, the police officers yelled.

On the other end of the road, Ojiji was running faster. He was headed for the part of the lagoon screened by trees. He figured that he could hide in the marshes awhile, then go round later to pick his Camry when the heat was off.

There was a single gunshot.

Ojiji fell.

He did not get back up again.

Hannu Afere is the author of *Digital Sìgìdì* (2020) as well as the editor of the *Anthology of West African Literature* (8th House, Montreal). When he is not writing, he can be found spending time with his dogs Rain and Karma. He writes from Lagos, Nigeria.

LESSONS FROM ESSAY LESSONS

Aisha Nelson

When the bell ends school's
petty prisons – rules, reasons –
Love and Life run out to play…

The sun finds it fun to generously pour its radiance through the window, onto a page of my exercise book. Perching at the top corners of the page are the constant Date and Exercise Number. Apart from these, this page is blank. And I know better than to expect that only these two, without writing the exercise proper, will fetch me a decent grade, an actual grade. I take time and care to write the topic and title of the new exercise. These two too, I know, still count for nothing. No grade.

Riza, my friend, has long finished and submitted her work – one of those essays.

I'm forever far from finishing mine. I can't even bring myself to begin writing. The thought of it:

"How I spent my Christmas Holidays"!

How I wish the sun fills my near-blank page – the whole of my exercise book, actually – with Words. With beautiful

Words. Beautiful but truthful Words. Words more truthful than they are beautiful. Many such words. Only such words. For I tell myself not to lie. All my essays, including this one, which I am even yet to write, really need to be short.

This is because all there is to think and write about my recent Christmas holidays can be done in as much as a single lean paragraph. Any addition will be unnecessary, superfluous – a smudge, even, on my integrity. Anything short of or more than the plain truth will be a grave lie. And to lie is something I am not to do, to not lie especially because of something as trivial as a grade, a better grade. So I believe.

Meanwhile, the street outside the classroom is bursting with so many stories outshouting each other for attention, shouting to be told, to be written, by anyone who cares to.

Ms. Enam Asimata will not be able to mark all the stories if every other pupil and I were to write a lot less than half of those stories. Yet, she complains my essays are too short. On the previous page of my exercise book is one such exercise. Her red ink's frozen scream under that last essay eternally reads,

> "*This essay is too short, Enam. This must be the last of this kind!*"

The last is long past. My turning over a new leaf is not only to write a new essay, but more importantly, to write one of appreciable length – at least, as deemed by my Class Six Teacher.

"No *offending* Ms. Enam Asimata this time," I tell myself.

So I set my Bic on the next and empty line of the page.

Slowly, I start. I finish my first sentence. But not without the expected drag. Little by teeny little, I write. And write on. One thoughtful word after the other, I fill the page with crisp, warm and fond pictures, moments and memories of my recent Christmas holidays. I am thankful to finally finish.

I shut my eyes for a few seconds. I let myself dream of seeing my new page – my whole book, and hopefully, my desk too – spill with the many words I very recently poured…

My essay is set. It sits still, clean and lean on the page. It sits still and still several lines shy and short of half the new page.

And even before Ms. Enam Asimata's red ink will later add its remarks and number grade about my essay, the blank larger half of the page screams the wretchedness of my mere scratch and funny toil of an essay. The scream rumbles and doubles. The scream fires and crackles sparks and thunders on my poor page. Methinks I even feel my desk quake with all the turmoil.

I watch on, helplessly, as the rumblings scatter my poor essay. The tongues of fires, they hungrily lick my already-lean and now-scattered essay away. Then the rumblings, now full and fat from eating my essay, sport a sly smile, give a guttural belch, wail one long yawn. Stretching its tiny limbs and making to take a nap on my page, the bloated ball of rumblings burst…

The mess from the burst splashes on my sad long face, spills over and into the rest of my book, hangs thick above my desk. My face falls. My head remains bowed in shame, a shame I can't readily account for.

Save my face I must. I sit. Upright. Still.

But I don't write. I can't bring myself to write. Not anymore. Not yet. Not again. Not for this essay.

I look outside from my desk by the classroom window. That side of the world is bubbling with hordes and weights of life-s and promises – stories. The stories on the street leap off everyone and everything. The stories wander frantic, peeping here and far and there and near, wearing fragile half smiles, prancing down and up some- and every-where. The stories tug along and bump into everyone and everything and themselves, begging and hoping, insisting and waiting. To be written. Or to be told. Or both.

To just put on the temporal…

> *Eager traffic lights and drowsy street lights*
> *blink dawn off their metal-gilded brows.*
>   *Towering bill boards and*
>   *patches of dew-studded grass glance*
>   *beneath and beyond themselves. With glee.*
>   *Low drones of engines from all ends*
>   *embrace distant hums of some church organ.*
>   *keen conductors*
>   *are tucked in windows of moving vehicles.*
>   *keener hawkers*
>   *outshout, outrun each other around*
>   *vehicles.*
>   *Breeze heaves past, weaving*
>   *through throbbing background and*
>   *noise.*

*Wind whistles through
kites tattered and tangled and caught up
tall on soulless poles.
　　Colour-filled smells of
　　breakfasts linger and vanish
　　in between the thick and
　　trickle of people and other.
Warm human
bodies and bottles of
chilled water and drinks and such
sweat with heat and cold and both.
Time ticks. Time fidgets under blankets of
humid air. Humid air hangs at every
end of the street.
　A quick push there. A shove.
　A crisp pull here.
　A crash. And then, a thud.
Skyscrapers stand scattered,
grinning their morning greetings to high clear skies.
Spells of rain showers
soothe and refresh and smooth
aches and wilts and frays.*

*Groceries:
sprout on trays and baskets and such,
grow under sheds and stalls – shades and shelters of all forms –
await mediated harvests…*

> *A*
> *shuffle hardens into a walk. A*
> *jog eases into a walk. A*
> *jog grinds into a saunter. A*
> *stop springs into a saunter. A*
> *stop revs into a run. A*
> *shuffle breaks into a run…*
>> *Souvenirs*
>> *shine anew on shelves in shops.*
>>> *Honks and horns*
>>> *screech each*
>>> *other to hoarse stops.*
>>>> *Sun peeps from behind*
>>>> *billowy clouds, sporting a white toothless*
>>>> *smile.*
>>>>> *The street is a pool of people, street is dotted*
>>>>> *with soft whirls. The street is awash with*
>>>>> *happy hues, street sways to its own music.*
>>>>>> *Last glimmers of neon lights*
>>>>>> *fade past early shimmers of glass doors.*

Good old Life glides past. Everywhere I look, stories abound.

And here I still am, sitting and thinking, labouring and wasting myself away, behind an essay which refuses to be written. I think harder by the seconds. I search and turn my memory, times and over, trying to find if there still is one tiny detail about my Christmas holidays that I may have forgotten.

Then, I can blow up this new detail with words from that Word Class we learnt in the last Grammar Class: Adjectives, they call it.

But then, there is my face to save and my teacher to make happy – and my-self too to make happy, since my teacher and I share a *namE. Enam.*

And this is how I also will outdo one of my Grande-Mother's many sayings: I will "kill three – not just two – birds with one stone."

Two years later, I'm in a new class in a new school, with a new teacher, having the same lesson – Essay Writing. The topic is Debate, this time.

I begin with an introduction, as Ms. Boakye has taught me, and as I best know how. I begin with an introduction which excellently express my side of the motion, and fully justify it. I combine truth and length well enough – or so I insist on believing. That introduction should please any teacher, who should in turn, reward this my *rare* – if not *unique* – feat, ever since I began writing essays in school.

But I was to be surprised: I've outdone myself and the normal.

My introductory paragraph alone is two lines short of one page. I scan it. I read it. I skim it. I re-read it. I revise it. I proofread it. I review it. And I end up with the same essay and introduction, with the same words and word count. For I find every word in there worth choosing, very much worth the inclusion.

And by so doing, I displease another teacher for the opposite of a previous offence: many an essay too short to be of good and use.

It's been many years since. If only I had understood those Essays as *Compositions*, I would not have thought of *too many words as Lie-s*.

And Oh! How I wish I had realized much earlier that *too many words* could as well be truth, beautiful truth.

Whether about the use of Adjectives or some other writer-ly style, one thing emerged from this whole experience: Modesty – not of the raw and rigid kind. I prefer to call it, Giftedness, or simply, *Gift*.

This *Gift*edness, It has never needed to save its owner's face. Rather, It feeds her imagination and fills the pouring of her creations, It sharpens her outlook and adds life-colour to the fountain of her imagination.

This *Gift*edness effortlessly is. It intimately knows.

Through words, this *Gift*edness unfurls and flares out worlds beyond the mere now, worlds populated with personality, worlds loosened from locale, worlds forever far from the mundane. It is at once an exclusive sanctuary for all things too wondrous for the eloquence of words. It is a universe of possibilities upon infinities.

This *Gift*edness has a unique gift for everyone who encounters It.

This *Gift*edness does not kill one, two, three or more birds with one stone. Rather, like birds, It is free to soar the endless realms of the worlds of Words, soar and explore without the fear of room or restraint, without any fear of any kind.

So I now soar and explore, I write my life-world away.

And while at it, I am all too glad to watch the sun generously pour itself into my bliss…

Aisha Nelson dreams, writes, thinks and lives in Accra, Ghana, where she is also a college teacher. Some of her writing was shortlisted by Erbacce Press; another won Akwantuo Writing's Harmattan Poetry Prize. More of Aisha's work has appeared in outlets including Kalahari Review, One Ghana One Voice, an Accra Theatre Workshop production of short plays, Munyori Literary Journal, a Writers Project of Ghana poetry anthology, Phillis Wheatley Chapter, Afreada, a Caine Prize short story anthology, Saraba Magazine, a curatorial art exhibition at KNUST, University of London's Prairie Schooner and Obsidian, a journal of Literature and Arts in the African Diaspora.

Also in Ga, Luganda, Kiswahili and other translations, *Aku the Sun Maker* is Aisha's first children's storybook. A manuscript of her collected short fiction, *Lens and other Stories*, won the Kofi Awoonor Literary Prize (2018).

Aisha shares some of her writing at Nu kɛ Hulu (Water and Sun) https://aishawrites.wordpress.com/

PITHING

Henneh Kyereh Kwaku

he held the frog
& called on us to look on—
the physiologist,
as he pierced, with a needle
through the center of its skull
it stretched its limbs
in surrender

all one hundred & eighty
of us touched it, probably
in places it would have resisted
had we not seized every
power it had, to protest

hours later,
it kicked, kicked, kicked.

DEAR LOVE OR A SHORT SPEECH ON RESILIENCE

Henneh Kyereh Kwaku

I would have loved to quote somebody great, somebody important, somebody wise—to begin this speech, but I begin anyway. I would have spoken of revolutions & the art of not giving up. I would have loved to speak of all the women & men who had to be sacrificed for Africa to be free. Of the men who had to set themselves on fire to light the spirit of the revolution. Of the women who had to bleed themselves to invoke the courage in their dying men. Of slave ships & ancestors. I would have loved to present to you *courage* neatly wrapped in words, songs & actions:

>*here's my fist, up.*
>*chant with me—*
>*bleed with me*
>*chant with me*
>*stand up, fist up!*

But I will speak of waist beads & my love for them, & them on my love. Waist beads say a lot more than I can say. They mean a lot more than I can mean. I know we could break apart tomorrow or even the next second but tell me another thing that has seen more breakings than waist beads. Tell me. Tell me another thing that has seen more fire, more hammering, more bending than waist beads. Tell me something. Something as graceful as waist beads. What symbol of a revolution stands stronger than waist beads? Sing a song, take a stand, raise a fist:

> *when one breaks,*
> *another takes place.*
> *there are no ranks—*
> *no lows & highs*
> *same chant, same song!*

Henneh Kyereh Kwaku is a poet from Gonasua in the Bono Region of Ghana. He is the author of *Revolution of the Scavengers*, selected by Kwame Dawes and Chris Abani for the APBF New Generation African Poets Chapbook Series. His poems/essays/hybrids have appeared in Lolwe, Agbowo, Tupelo Quarterly, Tampered Press, Poetry Society of America, Praxis Magazine, IceFloePress, Random Photo Journal, Lunaris Review, CGWS, New South Journal and elsewhere. Find him on twitter/IG @ kwaku_kyereh

CHI CHI VOICES

Novisi Dzitrie

I usually cross the street to grab lunch. Two balls of kenkey and a plate of well-peppered domedo. No matter what, a man lives by bread. And more money makes a man eager to look for more places to spend more. So, come payday, you will see me do the unusual: a drive through Oxford Street, a climb into Aburi Gardens, a stopover at The Tulip, or a dash to La Palm.

Payday is still fifteen long days away so I do the usual thing. I cross the street and perch in a corner inside the kenkey base. This place is nothing more than a roofed rectangular container of cement blocks, twelve quick strides diagonally. Four tables are arranged across the length, impeding brisk walking. There are two benches at each table so the sitting is face-to-face, which is fine if I am in familiar company; otherwise, I am doomed to exchange eye contact with strangers. The discomfort of such unwanted intimacy is heightened when I am not in the mood for a chat.

I do not miss the inscription above the door when I come here. Nobody can miss it. A straightforward motto in bold black paint on a white background: 'HOT Yε MLI'. The Accra woman has her way of stating her case without embellishment. This is one such statement which, milled mechanically into English, becomes 'HOT IS INSIDE'. Food served hot is just as well for my stomach. The first day I took my desk at the Kaya Insurance Company, coming here made my day. But when I got my first pay, I tossed up my car key – caught it mid-air, and looked away from the kenkey base. To Osu or to Aburi… with money in my pocket, I was the butterfly flitting after nectar.

One thing about coming here though is, no matter the weather, one senses immediately, that the inscription on the threshold carries more meaning than the advertisement of hot food. This feeling comes in a wave of heat that embraces the body at once. The windows are no good: they open to the airless rear of a huge building. Two noisy fans stir the air tiredly, blowing heat and creaking, turn by tedious turn.

My food is served. The usual. I down it, lick my fingers and belch. I wish I could have another round but prudence gnaws at me. One pesewa now makes a lot of difference. But what? I can get more domedo and borrow money from my wife. She won't deny me. She will only grumble. At worst, she will insult my manhood. In any case if she refuses to give me, I can take an IOU at the office. But this is no good option now. I have taken IOUs over the past three months. This time I must redeem some respect for myself, some modicum of honour before my colleagues. "Ah man taya sef! Man taya! Domedo too now be expensive, twiaa-kai!" I belch again and I can taste the bile of angst on my tongue.

I want to spit. I could vomit. Not that the food is bad. Not at all. It is good. Not that I will swear, here and now, a severance of my affinity for domedo. No. This is a delicacy I had for free as a child from my father's second wife, Maa Bee. "Oh peace be upon her soul." I always say this when I remember her rare kindness. Then I make the sign of the cross and repeat, "peace be upon her kind soul". Everything changed when Maa Bee passed away. She would often say I should take my studies seriously and that if I observe the world carefully I will come to understand why it does not always rain. Now I know, but I cannot understand why prices only go up, up… They never come down. I raise my head, sweating out the heat and discover a bearded man sitting opposite me.

I swear, I had been alone here in my corner. No one had been sharing this table with me. No one! Now this man with his beard disturbs my freedom. When and how he came to sit in front of me, without a sound, without the least perceptible shadow, I do not know. He is just here from God-knows-where, with a hard and burnt face covered in sheer bush, staring at me with neither a trace of history nor the prospect of a smile. He looks like one of those who belong to secret societies of high orders exclusive to strict adherents of the Mosaic Law. I should have joined one of these cults a long time ago. I have heard it said repeatedly how they knit networks to help one another financially.

I begin a quick scan of this man. The quality of his hat reveals itself: it is a lavish black fedora. I have no business looking him in the eye. I scan the rest of his body: neat suit and bow-tie. I conclude he belongs to the upper end of the contemporary Ghanaian middle-class. They say Ghana is now a middle-income country. I say apuuuuu, but be it so, I place myself in the middle of this middle-class so I can see anyone below or above me. I sweep my eyes across the spectrum of this class and I see clearly that this man is above me.

The man must have heard me talking to myself, for he starts to speak, "The system is hard, my brother." I am jolted. I hold onto the edge of the bench. "The system is in a precarious state. It's as though we have a noose tightening on our necks slow and slow. It's suffocating. It's choking. It's dire, my brother, dire, dire!"

"Mmmmhhh... ah!" I nod, urging him on, "you can say that again."

"Nothing is working. Everything is becoming expensive. I can hardly afford one piece of fish to balance the carbohydrate from the kenkey." He speaks like a well-read man. He must be a lawyer.

But wait... for a whole lawyer to be unable to afford fish is bizarre. Fried fish! Even with my predicament I just bought pork served in the delicacy of domedo. So we have gotten that bad? "Waaaaa look ooo..." I do not speak pidgin when I am talking to the learned, but I couldn't care less now. I mix the language: "If people like we sef dey suffer like this then just imagine those down there. Huh... waaaaa look."

I still feel like spitting but I check myself again and force saliva down my throat. "Ah, we need a revo!" I smack my lips and I feel the muscles on my face contract. I imagine my reflection in a mirror. "Corruption everywhere! School fees up. Electricity bills up. Water bills! Yesterday koraaa they announced another increase in fuel prices. Just look ooo! I parked my car at home today. I have to wait for my pay to buy fuel again. Huh!

Everything is in reverse. We must revolt. We need one hard hitting revo to put some sense into the kolikoli of the government. That is the language they understand. They must sit up or get out. And if they want, we will raise a Sub-Saharan Spring right here. We will take over Nkrumah Circle and rain fire on the government like they did in Cairo, Tunis, Tripoli... yes!"

The bearded man agrees with me. "Yes, yes, you're right." He says; thrusting his fists into the air before me.

I am completely... livid now. No, not livid. To describe my state as livid would create a shortfall in my emotions. I am *burst*. Just burst. Burst! The bearded man holds my hand and taps, taps, taps my knuckles with his thumb. My chest heaves. I huff. I puff.

"Take this, my brother," the man taps me to a pause, "take," he says, "write my number." He puts a pen and a piece of paper in my hand. "We must talk," he insists.

"I agree, yes, yes." I say.

"Manye, I finish ooo..." I look up and shout to Manye the kenkey seller.

"So where do you work, are you a lawyer?" I ask, turning back to the bearded man, but he is gone. "Oh how?" I exclaim. By Christ! The bearded man is gone just as he came, without the slightest perceptible motion. An indescribable force raises me from my seat only to leave me hunched over the table. I try to sit back immediately, but I stand and straighten myself instead, looking around the base from corner to corner. I see nothing but curious eyes staring at me. They are the kind of stares you get when, at an otherwise quiet meeting with your superiors, you let out an inadvertent fart. "...aaah!" I feel the paper in my hand and I look to be sure. It is there alright – the bearded man's number, in my handwriting. "...aaah!"

"Massa Odenke, everything okay? Your money is only nine cedis." Manye, the semi-literate kenkey seller, says to me. I think I hear a chortle in her voice too. By Christ! My mobile phone buzzes to save me from her question. Her eyes are still fixed on me, as if I am some stranger.

I take the call with a heavy breath, which I try to control. "Hello... hello..." The image of the bearded man holding my hand and tapping it comes back to me. I try to calm down. "Hold on, hold on, please..." I plead with the caller as I approach Manye. I put a fifty cedi note on her counter.

"Eiii... as for this one I don't have change ooo. You'll buy water?"

"Noooo." I reject the trap without blinking. There's enough water in my office and I must save the little pesewas that count in times of need.

"Then go and come. You big men always carry big money. I don't have change."

"Then give it to me. I'll bring your nine cedis later." I reply.

I am not ready to leave all my fifty cedis with Manye. I take the money and head for the exit without waiting for her to say yes or no. She knows my office. She knows I won't run away with her money. As I make my way out, I feel the weight of curious eyes on the back of my head, making it heavy like a bender's hammer. I look up at the afternoon sky to avoid the gaze of fellow pedestrians.

"Ahaa… sorry, hello, hello…" I try to get back to the caller but I am left with that piercing hum of a dead line. "Oh…" I touch my forehead. "What is wrong eh?" I wonder. "Nothing. I'm fine." I assure myself.

I get back behind my desk at the office. There is not much for me to do. I always make sure the bulk of my workload is attended to before lunch. It is unpleasant to hurriedly swallow balls of kenkey just because of piled-up work. Now, I wish time would just fly. A couple of emails drop in my inbox and I reply to them. There is a meeting scheduled for tomorrow. I put finishing touches to a report and forward it to my boss for presentation. That is what bosses do. You do the work and they take it and present to all manner of assemblies, courting and receiving applause and smiling for cameras. Then, it is ten minutes to five; time to go. I pack up and head out.

I take no mean steps down the Adabraka slope towards Nkrumah Circle. I must be fast to catch a trotro home, to beat the evening traffic. This way, I get to watch the Seven o'clock News. It is a forty minute journey to Teshie where I live but traffic jams make it a tiring hour-and-half. As I approach Vienna City, I enter into a maze of hawkers grabbing spots on the pavements for the night market. There is a chaotic buzz here already. When I have money and I do not want to suffer traffic, I enter Vienna City to have a chilled beer and amuse myself at the sight of young women ranging from the skinny, through plump, to big bottoms, posing and pretending to be sexy. Whenever I do this I arrive home late and boozed to the marrow. Naki, my wife, does not fail to complain. Sometimes she disallows me from sharing our bed, but I couldn't care less. I sleep in the sitting room.

Instead of heading to the Kaneshie Station, I come and stand under the Faanofa overpass. I want to save myself from further inconvenience. Sometimes it is better to go to the Kaneshie Station, but my instinct brings me to the overpass even though I may suffer jostling for an hour or more, in competition with other commuters, before getting a trotro. Today I seem to have gotten here early enough. I look around and see about seven other people waiting for buses. A trotro comes along with the mate screaming "Tema-Teshie-Nungua". I climb onto it. Two others follow me and we move away.

Trotros are not comfortable. If you have a problem, the trotro is the place to compound it. The last time I boarded one, my trousers got trapped in rusted metal and I got off with a torn bottom. All I could do was to curse the driver and his mate. They could not be bothered. They were off, rolling down the road, with their broken exhaust going tu-tu-tu-tu-tu... I remember I swore never to take trotro again but for this damn economy occasioned by this wicked government.

Now I wish my legs were shorter. The seats in this trotro are so close I have to keep my legs apart to free my knees from getting sore. I stretch my legs further apart, squeezing my co-passengers. The one on my left is a young boy returning from school who obviously would not dare complain. I wear a stern look. But the one on my right shifts uncomfortably and hits me. I turn towards him immediately and offer my apologies. "Sorry," I say.

"It's okay. Don't worry." The man says without looking at me.

"Oh it's you." Christ! I meet the bearded man again. "I planned to call you when I get home. My phone went off." I say to him, but he is not minding me, "But how come I didn't realize you were the one sitting by me all this while?"

The man glances once at me with knotted brows and turns away to call out to the mate, "Mate, Danquah-First bus stop."

I would have thought an educated man like him would say 'bus conductor'. The bus stops and he starts getting down before I could say anything else.

"I'll call you tomorrow," I say to him.

He gets off and we move on. Now I'm wondering whether that's not the bearded man I met at the kenkey base.

"It must be him. Or? It's him … It's him. It must be him. Maybe he's so tired he didn't want to talk."

A man in the front seat turns towards me, "My friend, you're making too much noise."

This bewilders me. "Are you talking to me?" I know he is talking to me, but I still wanted to see if he sized me up properly, relative to him.

"Yes you! You're not the only person in the bus. Let's have some peace. From Circle you've made noise saaaaa, why? You're wearing a tie, gentleman – fine, respect yourself!"

"What the hell do you mean?" I take him on straight away. "Who do you think you are? Do you know me? Nonsense! If it wasn't for your useless government I'd have been driving my car and not been in this trotro with you."

I did not hear the man talk again.

I arrive home at six-thirty, just as I wanted. Naki is at home too.

"What happened with the car?" Naki asks, alarmed.

"You could have said welcome before asking about the damned car."

"I came back to find the car parked. I thought you were home early. I got here at four thirty and I called your phone without success. So imagine my worry…" Bla bla bla… Naki is like that, unless she does not find an excuse to spark her tongue.

"My phone was off,' I said, 'Can I have something to eat?"

"So what happened with the car?"

"Naki, I don't have money. That's what happened to the damned car. Will you give me money? Can I just have my food?"

I walk to the kitchen. I serve myself and walk back to the dining table. All the while Naki is following me, blabbing.

"Naki, I need money," I say between mouthfuls, "Give me a loan." Naki is quiet now. She does not even stir. "Naki, I'm talking to you." I say, louder.

"When I asked you about the car, did you mind me?" she retorts.

"So what? You're retaliating? Fine. There's no fuel in the car. I need money to buy fuel. Give me four hundred cedis. I'll give it back to you when I get my pay."

"Why should I give you four hundred cedis?"

"Didn't you hear me? I said the fuel is finished."

"So you, what do you use your money for? You don't give chop-money. You don't pay water bills. You don't pay electricity bills. When was the last time you bought me a piece of cloth, Enoch? ..." Naki starts blabbing again.

"Naki," I cut in, though she does not stop talking. "Go and ask your government why my salary cannot buy me a month's fuel. You voted for them. Go and ask them."

I finish eating and go back to the kitchen. This time Naki does not follow me. I dump the plate in the sink, wash my hand and return to the sitting room. Naki is watching one of those Mexican soaps on TV.

"Naki, it's past seven-o'clock. I want to watch the news." I take the remote control and change to good old GTV.

"You keep behaving strangely these days."

"Oh what? Leave me to watch the news."

Naki and I are both quiet now.

In the morning, I find myself on the sofa in the living room. The last thing I remembered was watching the news last night. "God, I must have been damned tired. But Naki should have called me, huh?" It is six-o'clock. I should have been on my way to work by now, especially since I will be taking a trotro today, too. "Naki can keep her money. After all, what? I will survive." I jump into the bathroom. I am soaping up when I hear Naki call.

"Enoch…"

"Yes." I respond. Soap enters my mouth and I spit.

"I'm leaving. I left the money on your pillow."

"Oh okay. Thank you dear, thank you, I should see you before you go. Wait, let me check you out." I say.

"I'll see you in the evening. I'm late." Naki says and I hear the door slam behind her.

I step out with Naki's money in my pocket and drive away with speed. The residual fuel can take me some distance alright. I check the filling station at La, opposite the La beach, but I am waved away. No fuel. "Ah!" I end up at Danquah Circle and, again, no luck. An attendant here is kind enough to direct me to Airport Shell.

"There's fuel shortage in Accra ooo," he says, "they say government has no credit."

I check my fuel gauge and it is reading almost zero. It is seven-ten. I must be in the office by eight-o'clock. The meeting starts at eight-thirty. Now I have money but there is no fuel to buy in this country. I look the attendant in the eye and say to him, "We need a revolution!"

I don't know why this government continues to stretch my patience. "Damn!" I curse. "This government is really shit." I beat, beat my steering wheel and change gears.

"I will get there," I assure myself and zoom off.

I do not even get to Airport Shell before seeing the long queue spilling onto the road. I join the queue right at the entrance and my engine stalls. The fuel is really finished now. Not a drop left for a spark. I get out and push the car with one hand while steering the wheel with the other. It takes me 20 minutes from the entrance to the pump which is just 30m away. I'm sweating and my shirt sticks to my skin. Finally, my tank is filled and I drive away.

"This government is very annoying," I sigh and fish for the paper in my breast pocket.

This is illegal, but I take my phone and dial the number while managing to keep my eyes on the road. I could be arrested, I know, but I have done this a few times without suffering any problem.

"Hellooooo…"

But all I hear from the other end is, "Chi chi chi chi …" It unsettles me.

I try again, "Hello, hello…"

And again the response is, "Chi chi chi chi…"

I do not understand what is happening. I pull into the Ring Road. Not bad. I have made good time. I remove the phone from my ear to check that the number I dialed is correct. It is, but I re-enter the number, just to be sure. I just do it. If I am unsuccessful I will try again after the meeting. But now I hear a voice at the other end of the line. This is what I expected.

"Hello Mr. Odenke." The voice booms and echoes in my ears. "It was good meeting you yesterday."

It is the bearded man. I want to ask him how he got my name but he is not allowing me to talk.

"Now listen carefully," He says.

I enlarge my ears.

"I have initiated you into the Chi Chi Fraternity by the most sacred oath."

I am not sure whether I'm hearing properly. Even if I am, I still want to hear that again.

"Sorry ..." I try to interject but the man was bent on finishing his statement.

"You're now a Brother. Brother Odenke. So do as I say without fail." He proceeds with an elaborate set of instructions. I listen.

When he is done, he calls my name, "Mr. Odenke," he says, "remember, you don't have the option of failure."

I put the phone down on the passenger seat and I drive on, making plans and nodding to myself.

"... the Sacred Secretary, Grand and Fearful", I find myself saying. "... but this man? Why these warnings? He doesn't know me. I'll show him I don't joke with serious matters."

The meeting at the office is done by eleven o'clock. Strategic whatever, whatever! Always the same long talks. We were served some lousy food but I took it for two reasons: first, it means I get to save some money and second, I could spend the break time attending to the bearded man's matter. This is exactly what I do. I pull some A4 sheets from my printer, grab my pen and scribble away:

"Dear Sir,

This is to bring ample and definite notice to your decorated office that we of The Chi Chi Fraternity have decided upon the most sacred oath to mount the biggest ever protest against government on the democratic streets of Accra.

It is an unassailable decision to exercise our right to bark wo wo wo at the government for its crass nonsensical occasioning of hardship on Ghanaians. For this, we warn; ours is no mean fraternity to play with. We shall countenance no frustration from your office. Indeed, paralysis from the waist down shall be the least punishment if you dare us.

Find attached our chosen route and schedule.

Respectfully,
Brother E. E. E. Enoch Odenke
(For The Sacred Secretary, Grand and Fearful)"

I place the letter and attachment in an envelope and address it to The Inspector General of Police, Ghana Police Service, Headquarters, Accra. I dash to the Police Headquarters five kilometres away to deliver the letter. The car responds well, weaving through traffic with ease. I make the journey, to and fro, in twenty-five minutes. My mechanic tells me fuel is blood and he is right, very right. There's not much to do for the rest of the day. A few applications rest on my table: a man has lost both legs, another lucky next-of-kin is making a bounty claim on the deceased uncle … Christ! I pray time should just whizz by, and it does.

It is just as well that time passes quickly. We gave a two-week notice to the police, and I would say it was too much, but now we have just four days until the march. This is encouraging. Today is Sunday. I am at home and Naki has gone to church. I telephone the bearded man.

"The Sacred Secretary, Grand and Fearful," I address him by his full title as soon as he picks the call. I begin to bow too, but I realize I am bowing to the wall and I stop. "Your fellowship, your universal encompass, I salute your supreme soar." I begin to salute again, then realize that I am saluting the wall and I stop.

"Yes my able lieutenant, well and truly so. I hope you're gearing up for the march."

"Oh yes, I'm ready, but pardon me, another view of the matter agitates my mind. If we're going to have that many souls pouring onto the streets of Accra, a million and half souls, as you said, shouldn't we just stage an Occupy Movement using social media till the government is brought down? That is what the Egyptians did. It was on TV. Libya too; Tunisia, Ukraine… I'll create the Facebook page, Twitter too. It's easy."

"Brother Odenke, relax. I told you ours is no social media fanfare. Brother, revolutions are brought about by real souls. We are bringing together real souls: witches, wizards, spirits, ghosts, UFOs, fire eaters, storm gatherers; all in flesh and blood."

"Well …"

"Yes Brother Odenke, just be ready at the Trade Fair Centre, eight am. sharp. You'll make a speech at the rally before the march."

"Okay, my Sacred Secretary, Grand and Fearful! I trust you." We end the call.

Finally the day for the march is here. I'm ready by five-forty. I'm clad in red and I imagine my eyes red-hot; no nonsense!

"Enoch, I need my money." Naki comes demanding.

"Ah! Ah!" Why God sends Naki to tempt me now, I do not know. I refuse to mind her, the devil.

"Enoch, I say I need my money."

"Okay, I hear. I'm going."

I start walking away.

"No, wait," Naki stops me, "Where are you going, dressed shabbily like this? Who's dead? Are you not going to work today? Is that not … let me see, oh Enoch! You cut my funeral cloth for a wrist band? Why? Why?" Naki is holding my hand and inspecting me as if I am her child. "… and where are you going?"

"I'm going to, no, we're going to put sense into the kolikoli of your good-for-nothing government. Next time don't vote for a useless government." I storm out of the house and start my march right away. This way, I can create more awareness carrying my placard: 'WICKED GOVT. MAN TAYA!!!'

I sweep the length and breadth of the Teshie-Nungua road as I make my way towards the Trade Fair Centre, La. I scale the heights of ramps, circumvent the circumferences of potholes with deliberate arced advances or, if put to the challenge, I cut across their diameters with turbo-strides. My march is brisk but I make sure everyone – the hawkers, people passing in vehicles, those just waking up, just everyone – even kiosk-owners dotted along the road – can read my placard. I am holding it aloft and I can feel how large it spreads out on the road, aided by the breeze from the sea a hundred metres away to my left.

Drivers blast their horns at me to allow them to pass and I shout as I march: "Yes! This is it. Government shall fall today. Tsoooooboi-ya! Heya! Tsoooooboi-ya! Heya!"

I am almost at the Trade Fair Centre. My ears start picking up the sound from the gathering of the million-and-half souls.

It is getting louder and louder. This is exciting. I start to jog/run, run/jog. Then I begin to hear, "There he is, there he is. Enoch! Enoch! Hold him, hold him."

This is pleasing to the ears. I am jogging/running, running/jogging; even faster. Not many people get this appreciated for their efforts. My organizational skills have clearly paid off.

"Hold him, hold him," I hear them say.

About a million hands grasp me at once and bundle me up like I am a trophy. I look around for The Sacred Secretary, Grand and Fearful. I try to pick out those with long beards. He's nowhere to be found. Instead, I see Naki in the crowd, screaming. I see her mouth move yabi yabi yabi but I cannot tell what she is saying.

I scream back at her: "Naki, ahaaaa! You see? Naniama! Now you see sense!"

They carry me away.

Novisi Dzitrie was born to Ghanaian parents in Kakata, Liberia. He lives in Ghana and volunteers at the Writers Project of Ghana. His writing appears in Obsidian, SAND Journal, New Orleans Review, Prairie Schooner and Saraba Magazine. Others have been included in the Writers Project of Ghana's anthologies *Look Where You Have Gone To Sit*, and *According to Sources*.

BACK TO SEEDS AGAIN

Samuel Alesu-Dordzi

"Effective today, all persons are required to stay home until the lockdown is lifted. Persons who fail to do so will have themselves to blame," Jinga heard the president say on radio. Jiri, his only son rushed to him and asked "J, I have heard that the president is asking everyone to stay home. What is happening? Does it mean I can't go and play anymore?"

Jinga looked at his worried son and responded, "Yes, for now. We have just become seeds again."

We have become seeds again. This was not something that Jinga thought he would hear himself say again, so soon after he had last spoken them. "Seeds again."

Until recently, Jinga had been a professional banker who had a good and contented life. He had all the things that a person in the middle class could boast of. And he could afford the occasional outing to fancy restaurants. He loved life. It was just that life just didn't love him back. For if life did, what could explain his wife's sudden disappearance from his life? And the recent streak of bad luck that had come his way?

He preferred not to recount the story behind his recent job loss. He had convinced himself that nothing happened. In the same week in which he lost his job, he came home one day to find that his house had been ransacked. He filed a complaint with the police but he knew in his heart that nothing was going to come out of it. All the negative things that could possibly happen to a human being were happening.

Since his wife ran away, he had taken a liking to a woman in his office – Estelle. Jinga and Estelle were both employed into the bank in the same year. So, by default, they were quite close. They discussed work related challenges. They gossiped about their bosses. But they also undermined each other in very strange ways. Jinga for instance had previously told his superiors about how Estelle was always on her phone when she was supposed to be working. Estelle had in turn told Kusi, Jinga's direct superior, with whom it was widely rumoured that she was having an affair, that Jinga had told her that he was better than Kusi and could easily do his job. In spite of the backstabbing, they both shared some sense of admiration for each other. One weekend, Jinga went unannounced to visit Estelle at home. And there was Kusi, eyes fixated on some television programme. If Jinga had seen him first, he would probably have walked away. But no. familiarity caused him to slip. He had been to Estelle's place on so many occasions that he had convinced himself that that was his second home. He typically did not knock before he entered, and that was what happened on that day. And there was his superior – in a T-shirt so tight that it would have been a matter for real debate about who was struggling: the T-shirt or its owner. Estelle was not in the room, maybe she had sensed the clash and was hiding, waiting, looking out for what might possibly happen.

The stares that the two men gave each other were a story by themselves. This was the kind of situation that you would often see between two dogs. What each of them thought was a safe territory wasn't, after all. But Jinga knew one thing: a lot rose and fell on this occurrence. His monthly remittance to his parents depended on this. The payment of his water and electricity bill depended on this. The payment for the little luxuries in life depended on this. He could have just walked away with his tail between his legs, but he was not the kind to run away. He convinced himself that whatever was happening had very little to do with work.

It was a tense situation, and it did not end well. From the beginning, the conversation was tinged with belligerence.

"Don't you have a wife and children?" Jinga asked.

Kusi could not help but respond, "What do you mean? You useless boy." He continued, "I know you think you are better than me. We shall see…"

Still, there was no sight of Estelle. She must have been hiding in the kitchen or washroom.

Finally, Kusi shouted, "Get out of here!" Jinga left. For a moment, he wondered why he even stepped out. He felt he lost the game.

The days following the incident were tough. Nothing he did was enough. He was always on the chopping board. But when news of a pending redundancy first slipped into the staff working area, he knew that his end had come.

And he was not wrong.

All he could see when he read the letter was "Foolish man, next time you will stay in your lane." He knew that all the talk about the need to improve efficiency was just nonsense. He had dared to call his superior a fool and he paid the price for it, short and simple. Estelle had never called nor approached him since the day of the fight. She always found a way of avoiding Jinga.

She might have made a choice between Jinga and Kusi, or she was just looking out for herself. After all, she had got her life to keep. Or, just maybe, Kusi was keeping a keen eye on the two of them.

This was not Jinga's first job.

He had formerly worked as a teacher. Always passionate, he had stuck his neck out for the things he believed in. He believed in fairness and justice. These were things he had learnt from his grandmother, who had raised him up to speak up against wrongs in society. His 89-year grandmother had once publicly called out the chief in the village for selling the same piece of land to four different persons. There were discussions and rumours of her being banished. But that never happened.

So Jinga learnt how to speak out by watching his grandmother and this virtue stayed with him. But while Jinga's grandmother had the good fortune of getting away with speaking up, Jinga did not. And in moments when he was lost in thought, he would always whisper to himself, "me and my big mouth."

However, his first posting as a teacher was also his last. He was overly dedicated and committed, which made him the object of ridicule by his colleagues. He organised extra classes for the students at no cost to them. He led extra-curricular activities in the school. He would often visit the students at home over the weekend and interact with their parents. As a result, he developed strong bonds with the students, and soon they began to confide in him. Some told him about teachers who were pestering them for sex and marriage, which led to Jinga confronting the teachers and reporting them to the headteacher – until he discovered that the headteacher was one of those harassing the students. He confronted the headteacher over this.

It was a nasty encounter.

Next thing he knew, he had been charged with insubordination, and even more seriously, with sexual harassment. Nothing he said in his defence seemed to change anything. The headteacher alleged that Jinga had issued a death threat over a girl that Jinga was sleeping with.

It was a well-crafted plot to destroy his career. Under pressure from her parents, the chief of the village and the headteacher, she told a disciplinary hearing that Jinga had in fact asked for sex and to get him off her back, she lied to him about having an affair with the headteacher.

This was not how Jinga expected things to end.

But that was how it ended. His record was tainted.

And so he re-invented himself, as it were. He had his shady connections change his name and issue him with a fake birth certificate and other documents. It was such a desperate decision, but there was no way he could get any job in teaching, or any respectable job, with that in his background.

Jinga had always feared that the story of his past would come back to haunt him. But he felt that was the price he had to pay for speaking up for the supposedly underprivileged. And here he was, having to live with the guilt of forged certificates and identity documents. But, he convinced himself, the forgery was only to the extent that it allowed him to have a change of name. Going through the official channels to change his name would mean that he had to acknowledge his old name as well. But he did not want any of that. He had trained his mind to distance himself from his previous self. And he seemed fairly successful.

When the man he had contracted to get him the forged documents completed his work, the soft-spoken elderly crook said to him, "You were planted as a seed. It is time to germinate again." These words always remained with him. In hard times, he would tell himself – I have been planted again. That was the only way he could rationalise it. He had been planted again. He was just waiting for that moment to germinate. To shoot up. To rise again. It was just a matter of time, he said to himself. He had been through worse. Being declared redundant was not the worst thing to have happened to him. But it brought out his worst fears, and all the uncertainties of the past.

He had managed to get a job with the bank with a fake document. But who knew this? Who knew? This was a secret only two people knew. Estelle. And his estranged wife.

Only those two people knew.

Samuel Alesu-Dordzi is a lawyer and a writer. He has for the past decade served as a columnist with *The Mirror* and has pioneered a number of writing initiatives such as the Ghana Law Hub and the Criminal Law Reports of Ghana.

FAILINGS OF A NATION

Ikechukwu Nwaogu

Ousmane Traore was in a foul mood. He had woken up before the first cock crow, washed his face and hands in the harsh cold, and set out for work. It was a routine he was used to, one he had maintained for the past three years. The village's sole transport, a rickety old bus with the ironic name, 'Safe Journey', would be arriving soon, and being late could mean having to stand throughout the one-and-half-hour trip to his job at the Federal Abattoir, Kukere. Worse still, it could mean hanging precariously by the door as the bus bumped and skittered over the potholed roads. He had woken up to the rumbling of his stomach, a stark reminder that he had not eaten the previous day, and unless something good happened, there would be a few more hungry nights to come. He might even have to borrow again to get by.

That morning everything seemed to be working against him. While still too dark to clearly discern faces, he had walked the mile separating his house from the park. By the time he arrived at the park, dawn had broken and a few other commuters had arrived and stacked up their goods for the trip.

"Ousmane!"

He turned towards the caller. Bubar waved to him and started up the hill towards the park. A short, swarthy man with hands like tree branches and a face only a mother could love, Bubar was a lout who made a living by working for people on their farms during the planting season. He was prone to violence, and people preferred to stay out of his way. He was also into debt collection and was often employed to recover debts for a commission. As Bubar approached, Ousmane's heart sank. He wondered who had sent Bubar to him. It was never a good sign for Bubar to be looking for you, first thing in the morning.

"Bubar, good morning," he said, when Bubar came close enough.

"What is good about the morning? Ehn, tell me, what is good about the morning? I've been looking for you. For the past three days, I have been coming to your house, but each time your wife said you had gone. Today now, I woke up early, and came to your house, but you had gone again. I had to run all the way here so I could get you before the bus left."

"Ah, I'm greeting you now, is that a bad thing?"

"Please, keep your greeting. Abdoulai said you're owing him money, is it true?"

"Err… em… It's not quite like that."

He drew nearer, as though Ousmane were preparing to run off. "Four thousand naira," he shouted, "you say it's not like that, how is it like?"

"I… er… I borrowed two thousand from Abdoulai, but before then I was owing Alhassan 2,500, so after I paid Alhassan five hundred, it was now remaining two thousand, then Alhassan's mother-in-law died, and as I did not have money to give him, I asked Abdoulai, and Alhassan was owing Abdoulai 2,000, so I was now... "

"My friend, don't waste my time, whether it is two thousand or four thousand or twenty-eight thousand, Abdoulai said I should collect it from you, so where is the money?"

"Emm... Let me explain... see, I don't – " he began.

Bubar cut him off. "You don't what? Where is it?"

A crowd had started to form around them, bored passengers waiting for the bus who were only too happy for the diversion.

"I don't have money right now, maybe by month end I will – "

"Look, you are not serious," Bubar shouted, grabbing a fistful of Ousmane's shirtfront. "You must pay me that money today, because you have been dodging me since. How long is it now? How long? For the past three months you've been owing that money, saying the same thing, month end, month end, when month end comes, you disappear, and after you say you don't have money. Do people enter bus without money?"

As if on cue, the rumbling of the bus could be heard as it trundled over a hill and approached the park.

"Please now, the bus is coming, and I'm already late. I will see you this evening, once I come back, just let me –"

"Kai! You think I'm playing? Don't let me show you my red eye oh! That money, it must come out today, whether you like it or not. Were you planning to give the driver sand, or one of your dirty teeth as money? Give me something!" he pulled and twisted the shirtfront in his grip even tighter. The crowd began to disperse as commuters drifted towards the approaching bus.

Those with bags of produce or other luggage began to heft their load, ready to board the bus.

"Please, please, let me go, the bus is here already, and I'm going to be late. I will see you this evening without fail," Ousmane pleaded.

"Give me something first, I cannot come all this way for nothing, at least let me buy some gin to wash my mouth this morning."

Searching his pocket, Ousmane came up with a dirty twenty naira note. "Please this is my last money, at least let's share it, so that I can have some money to take transport back home, please, please now."

Releasing the shirt in his grip, Bubar hissed contemptuously and snatched the note from quavering fingers. From a wad of notes he pulled out of his pocket, he extracted a tattered ten naira note. He handed Ousmane the money and growled, "This evening o! Don't forget!"

But Ousmane was already chasing after the departing bus, waving frantically to catch the passengers' attention. A skinny old man in the back of the bus waved him on: the passengers had seen him, but the bus could not stop yet. They were going uphill and the ancient bus needed all the momentum to crest the hill. He ran on till the vehicle trundled to a stop at the top of the hill, where it idled, waiting for him. The conductor jumped down and wedged a rear tyre with a wooden block. He was a scraggly youth, with a face pitted and cratered by acne. He was wearing a shirt that might once have been white but was now such a mish-mash of stains and dirt that it could answer to no particular colour. As Ousmane jogged towards the bus, the conductor yelled, "Do quick na, we go sleep here?" He hissed angrily as Ousmane boarded the bus. He struck the side of the bus and yelled, "Carry go, carry go joor!" Then he reached down and pulled out the block.

Ousmane squeezed himself between the skinny old man and a fat woman carrying a child. The child was crying pitifully, and every now and then, the woman unfolded the edge of her wrapper and wiped its runny nose. Yet, almost as soon as she did so, it began to run again, like a small stream fed by a spring in the child's head. As the bus began to roll forward, the conductor began his rounds, collecting fares from the passengers.

Ousmane was lost in thought when the conductor got to him, so when the fat woman nudged him, he started violently and scowled at her. "Wetin? Why you dey push me?"

"Abegi bring your money before you begin dey find quarrel," said the conductor.

"How much?" he asked, patting his pockets left and right.

"See oh! Na today? When you de enter this motor before, na person de pay for you? Give me the money joor!" He hissed again, a sound that came out remarkably well, considering that he was missing two front teeth, with many others in various stages of decay. Ousmane fiddled in his pockets for the money, inadvertently brushing an arm against the woman beside him.

"Oho! you dey pretend say you dey find your money, come dey touch my breast abi? Shameless man, no go marry! Abeg commot your useless hand from here! No dey touch-touch another man wife!"

"See me see wahala, how I take touch your breast?" He hissed, "I don marry oh, abeg pack your breast keep for that side, no dey throway am everywhere." He laughed a little too loudly.

He brought out the ten naira note and slapped it into the conductor's hand, receiving a five naira note in return, which was its equal in decrepitude. He put the money in his shirt pocket. The skinny old man on his left tapped him and leered at the woman, then winked at him. Ousmane was smiling back before he realized that the old man thought he had jostled the woman intentionally. He saw other passengers grinning and checked himself.

As if on cue, the bus jolted over a particularly rough spot. The fat woman's baby woke up and started bawling. She wiped off the mucus from the baby's nose and flicked it inadvertently on his shoe. He pretended not to notice. He didn't want any other confrontation with her. Besides, the shoes were battered and scuffed, having suffered on various roads, and at the hands of too many cobblers; what more could a little blob of mucus do?

A man opposite him sneezed. The spray misted his face, his shirt and his eyes. He began to imagine that he could smell it in his nose and taste it in his mouth. He almost yelled but thought better of it. The man could easily pass for Bubar's elder brother and Ousmane was in such a mood as to endure every affront with dignity. The man fished out a dirty handkerchief and applied some more grime to his face: Ousmane could not imagine the rag being used to *clean* anything. As the man mopped his face, he said a condescending "sorry" to Ousmane who nodded in acknowledgement. Soon afterwards, the man began to flare his nostrils, as though warming up for another sneeze. Ousmane swiftly vacated his seat, to hang by the door of the bus. The conductor plonked down into Ousmane's seat, just in time to be sprayed by the man's sneeze.

The conductor let loose a string of curses. Provoked, the man threw a blow but the nimble lad dodged out of the way and the blow hit the fat woman. The man tried to throttle the conductor, the fat woman tried to throttle the man, and finally the bus creaked to a halt as the driver hurried down to save his boy.

Ousmane looked around him as the quarrel escalated. The conductor's mouth was now bleeding. The sneezing man had scratches on his face – as if the scars from his tribal marks were not injustice enough – and the woman's eye was puffy and red. Ousmane pulled out the cheap digital wristwatch he kept in his pocket. He checked the time and put the single-strapped timepiece back in his pocket. He was clearly going to be late today, and the quarrel showed no sign of ending.

He remembered the Health Inspection officer, Mr. Jenkins, castigating the other staff on a previous occasion. "Just imagine," he had thundered, "most of you come to work so late, and that's from the staff quarters. Yet Ousmane gets here by 8 o'clock. How many of you know where he stays? Very far! Yet he makes this journey to Kukere every day, come rain, come shine, and still comes in before most of you. In fact, I have decided to give him an apartment in staff quarters. And some of you will have to look for a place to stay, so that you can justify your criminally late arrival at work. And maybe you can find jobs closer to your home there as well!"

Abruptly, Ousmane got off the bus. He was still a long way from his regular stop, but he figured he could get to work faster if he walked. "Na here you dey drop before?" asked the old man.

"I dey for hurry," explained Ousmane, "and before them go settle quarrel finish, e go don late. Make I take leg dey hurry dey go."

"Ah, this work serious oh, you no fit late small?" joked the old man as Ousmane walked away.

Ousmane walked briskly. He looked back at the stationary bus as he breasted the next hill and nodded at the wisdom of his decision to proceed on foot. He walked fast, raising puffs of dust with each step, until he kicked against a stone and almost fell. He looked back at it and swore. He might have been less fervent in his oaths had he known that the 'stone' was in fact one of the last uneroded portions of the original roadwork. He had actually been tripped up by the road. He squatted by the roadside and pulled off his shoe to inspect the damage. Presently, he heard a noise and looked up just as the bus rumbled past, the expressions on the faces of the passengers ranging from amusement to contempt. He looked around for a cobbler and, finding none, put on his shoe and resumed his journey, at a slower pace and with a shuffling gait.

As he rounded a bend in the road and entered Kukere, he knew instinctively that most of his colleagues would have arrived before him. The complimentary speech from Mr. Jenkins would not be forthcoming that day. He looked at his shirt, once clean and tucked in, but which now bore the relics of his journey: the hands of Bubar, the unwashed bodies in the bus, the dust from his trek, and his own sweaty body. His trousers, thick with the dust from his trek, flapped as he walked towards an itinerant cobbler under a ficus tree just off the road.

Ousmane took off the shoe and handed it to him for appraisal.

"Ten naira."

"Wetin? Abeg, na two naira."

"Kai mana."

They haggled back and forth until the price was finally set at three naira. While the cobbler worked, Ousmane thought about the woman on the bus, and mentally compared her to his own scrawny wife, who was pregnant and almost always sickly. As soon as the cobbler finished, he paid him, put on his shoe, and hurried off. The time was a quarter to nine.

As he entered the squat, ugly building that was the Federal Abattoir, an inner door opened, and Mr. Jenkins emerged, puffing on a foul-smelling cigarette.

"Well, well, and what have we here, if it isn't the boss himself?" he sneered.

"Good morning, sir."

"And a very good morning to you too, Ousmane. Do you know what the time is?"

Ousmane knew better than to pull out his watch. He stuttered, "Sir, the bus… my shoe got spoilt on the road and I had to stop and fix it… "

Mr. Jenkins gave him a feral grin. His teeth were discoloured from tobacco smoke. He was tall, abnormally so, and skeletally thin, something the cigarettes he chain-smoked all day did nothing to alleviate.

"There's mail on your desk," he dropped the butt of the cigarette on the floor and stepped on it. "I suggest you read it very carefully, as it contains very important information for you." Without looking at Ousmane, he walked away.

Ousmane got to his desk in the Records Department. He blinked in surprise at the telegram. Quickly he opened and read it through with shaking fingers.

GREETINGS STOP SCHOOL ON STRIKE STOP NO MONEY STOP MANAGING AT CONSTRUCTION SITE STOP SEND FUNDS URGENTLY STOP WILL RETURN HOME STOP PLEASE PLEASE STOP ADAMU STOP

He closed his eyes. It was for this reason he slaved and toiled; it was for this reason he had only one pair of shoes, for this reason he scrimped and scraped. He had two threadbare trousers, four ragged shirts, a sickly, pregnant wife, and a malnourished child. He winced at the thought of his younger brother coming home, another mouth to feed, more clothes to buy, more expenses… and he had sworn on their father's deathbed that Adamu would finish school. He began to sweat.

There was a low hum as the power supply to their office was restored and the rickety fan hanging from the ceiling began to turn. Undoing the top two buttons on his shirt, he leaned forward to begin the day's work.

That was the moment the fan broke. A relic of the colonial era, it was just another symbol of the abandonment into which the whole country had fallen. It had been squeaking for years as the crossbeam to which it was affixed steadily deteriorated, as much due to stress as to the activities of woodlice and termites.

As the fan came crashing down, one of the spinning blades caught Ousmane on the side of his head. The blade struck him broadside, knocking him unconscious, rather than killing him. The fan crashed into his desk, breaking it and pinning him underneath. Two ripped wires from the ceiling touched, causing a loud bang and a shower of sparks. As the other clerks began to scream, Ousmane recovered consciousness and struggled weakly to free himself of the debris. His eyes fell on the telegram on the floor beside him, and he groaned as he tried to decide if he was lucky, or unlucky, to have survived.

Ikechukwu "Eye Kay" Nwaogu is a writer, editor, and ghostwriter based in Ogun State, Nigeria. Born in Lagos and raised all over the country, he credits his parents for teaching him to read, and his siblings for teaching him to write. From radio drama to short stories, flash fiction to screenplays, and the odd book review or ten, he has tried them all, constantly seeking to stretch himself and find expressions for his art. In 2017, Strange Horizons UK interviewed him in their "100 African Writers of Speculative Fiction" series. In 2018, his novella, *The Book of Lost Words*, was a finalist at the inaugural edition of the GTB/Okadabooks/Farafina Dusty Manuscript contest. He is an alumnus of the prestigious Ebedi International Writers Residency, Iseyin, and the Africa Speculative Fiction Society/British Council Writing Workshop. His interests are writing and Gregorian Chants. He is presently at work on a novel.

A WALKER (IN THE CITY)

Sarpong Kumankoma

Each speck of dust
on my feet is a reminder
of every single soul
awaiting my return
as their messiah.

The cracks on my heels
map out the paths
I have travelled in search
of the paradise
I promised.
I—a saviour
—am in need of salvation
but I remain a miracle
worker raining down
manna from my hunger.

The paths I have taken
are across many rivers
of tears and sweat—
a web of guilt and regrets
with a few faded spots of joy

So, while I still walk through
this hell'ven (with hope beneath
my feet) toward a triumphant
return to my people,
should I stumble on your feet
do not crucify me!

Sarpong Kumankoma won the first prize in the inaugural edition of the Kofi Awoonor Literary Prize. He is currently training to become a veterinary surgeon.

WAITING FOR MARTHA

Elizabeth Johnson

Every night, we sit on the bare floor in the dark, somewhere in the forgotten parts of Accra, eating the same meal. Mother still gets dinner ready for four. It is always hot inside our new house: two kiosks merged into one just opposite the place we used to call home. Father eats in silence, his eyes avoiding everyone. I have become accustomed to his sighs as his lips part to welcome the stale morsels of kenkey with pepper. Mother fakes an appetite and pretends to eat, but the smell of alcohol and meat gives all her secrets away.

Earlier this afternoon, the man on the radio was yelling into the microphone about the government's housing projects, which were 'rescuing' displaced Ghanaians from the slums. He sounded like an energetic market preacher yelling at the crowd despite his microphone. I imagined he was as chubby and dark as Mr. Donkor, mother's new lover.

It had not taken long for everyone to know about mother's affair. Mr Donkor was the taxi driver who brought mother home the day she fled the house and caused a scene at the market. That was the day it all began, the affair and father's drink addiction. It is hard for me to remember that once upon a time we lived a different life. In my young years, I have heard adults speak of change in similar ways. They say it does not come suddenly, that it starts slowly and picks up pace until it has happened. But our change came suddenly.

We lived humble lives, my father, mother, sister and me. Our parents taught us to mind our business and wish no one harm. My mother was a good listener, sighing with her fellow women when they sighed, hissing when they hissed and laughing when they laughed. My father was a simple man who lived within his means. He loved a cold bottle of Guinness and spent his free time telling my sister, Martha and I stories from his younger years. He told us tales he hoped would stay with us when we were older and he was not around to give us the advice we needed. Sometimes, I would ask Martha the meaning of a word father used but she would laugh at me and remind me that I was the smart one going to school to become the medical doctor, the one destined to raise our social status.

My sister Martha meant everything and more to me. The ten-year gap between us was filled with love and a bond so strong. I admired and respected her, the way she helped mother in the market, the way she had not argued with father when he suggested that she quit school so that I could continue. I would look at her in awe as she struggled to help me with my homework or fight off the older boys when they bullied me. She was almost perfect – almost, because she did get angry with me sometimes. Even then, I would always remind myself that my sister loved me and would protect me even at the cost of her own life…

Yet, now there are many things I am not so sure of.

Six months ago, the men with their bulldozers and matching yellow PPE overalls came. Without saying a word they tore it all down; my father's dreams, his hard work, his toil and dedication. I remember rushing home to show my family my school report card, my feet gathering speed as my excitement grew. I was looking forward to Papa's pat on the back, the same way he greeted his friends when they said something that touched him. I was looking forward to my mother's dance and her sugar bread treat, and to Martha's warm embrace, and her ice cream treat.

It had been a hard term, but I had stayed dedicated to the goal of topping my class. It was my only way of appreciating my family's sacrifices for me. We lived in an uncompleted house. I was too high in the clouds to notice the dust rising from our unplanned neighborhood.

I noticed the men with their bulldozers and yellow overalls, and the people packing the remains of their belongings. I did not stop to listen when my friend, Kwame, tried to catch up with me, to warn me.

Then I reached our street, and to the remains of what had been home. Without notice, they had torn it all down: my father's dreams, his hard work and dedication. Our uncompleted house had been reduced to debris without any warning. Report card still in hand, I watched as mother tried to console the weeping man who I could barely recognize as my father. While mother begged him to pull himself together, tears running down her own face, Martha gathered what she could of our belongings. It was three hours later before mother finally convinced father that it was better we left to find a decent place to sleep. As we moved silently, everyone – especially Martha – avoided my eyes.

Along with several other families, we spent the night in the auditorium of the Presbyterian church. Families huddled together. It was a long night with my mother and other adults bargaining for hours with the pastor. Eventually, after appeals from his young wife, the pastor accepted the five-cedi-per-head charge for the night. It was mother who paid. Father had not said a word.

I remember waking Martha up that night to take me to pee. We walked in silence the whole time while I searched for a good spot. Martha did not hold my hand like she always did. She did not walk ahead of me either. On our walk back to the auditorium, I realized that I still had my report card in my pocket. I decided to show it to her. She was always the first person to see it, anyway. It was a secret we shared. Later, when our parents called her to have a look, she would pretend to have seen it for the first time and be excited all over again...

'Maybe this will make everyone happy,' I whispered, unsure if she heard me. The damaged streetlight was hanging half-way down and flickering every other second. Martha took the report card from me. She stared at it vacantly, as if seeing one for the first time in her life. Then she burst into a frenzy that horrified me, as she ripped the card into a million pieces.

With so much violence, I was more afraid that she would hurt her fingers than concerned about my report, but she watched, satisfied, as the last pieces of the card fell to the ground.

Then, with barely a glance at me, she made her way back to the church auditorium, not bothering to see if I followed.

As Martha walked away, the flickering streetlight made her appear and disappear, until she faded away completely, and I was all alone. I realized then that the men with the bulldozers had destroyed not just my home but my family... they all seemed out of their minds, in a trance. I gasped, realizing that I had been holding my breath all the while. I stood still, allowing myself to adapt to the new nakedness the cold night breeze brought to me.

These days, I spend my time as my father's keeper, making sure that he returns when he goes out for a drink or some air. Sometimes, when mother starts to talk to herself again, he would step out. I would find him on the land that once was our home, the land that was now turning into another luxurious apartment project that would likely stay empty when completed. Sometimes, I would speak to him in the hope that he would respond, but he never does. He would simply follow me to our new kiosk house when I told him it was time to go, or hand me the money when I offered to get his drinks for him.

I think about Martha a lot. I wonder where she is and what she is doing and if she thinks about me, about any of us. I realize I never really knew my sister. I did not know what she wanted for herself, the things she liked and the things that made her sad. Although I am upset she left me, I sometimes pray for her.

Five months ago, as we ate our kenkey with leftover pepper from the day before. Martha decided that mashing her kenkey was a better option and so she proceeded to do so, her tin of milk and groundnuts sitting by her. I could tell from the way mother eyed her that she wanted to ask how she could afford things like milk, groundnuts and mosquito coils. But we had all learnt to stay out of everyone else's business.

As I watched Martha skillfully turn her hard ball of kenkey into a smooth paste with the knife in her cup, our eyes met and she smiled at me for the first time in months. It took a while to register that expression, and the fact that my sister was communicating with me. Ever since the night incident at the church, she had not looked once in my direction. She had become a new person since then, staying out many nights at a time and coming home only to take a bath. Sometimes, she fought with mother when Mr. Donkor came around. Sometimes she threw father's drinks away. It had become so bad that I preferred the days she was not home. Yet, now I could feel my body respond to the smile, my hair standing as we kept eye contact. At that moment I believed that somewhere behind that hardened face my sister was still there, although distant and unreachable.

As we stared at each other, the illegally connected lights went off. Mother asked Martha to go get candles without giving her any money, but Martha was already on her feet and heading out of the door. I remember her hand squeezing mine, the way she used to do when she had something special to give me. I remember the crack of moonlight entering the house as Martha made her way out, slowly at first — as if waiting for a sign — and then finally she vanished.

The kenkey hardened in the cup, the milk soured in the tin, the groundnuts spoiled, Martha did not return. It has been five months and she has still not returned.

Elizabeth Johnson is a Ghanaian-Nigerian writer and researcher. Her stories, both fiction and nonfiction have been published on a few online platforms. In 2019, she won 3rd place prize for the Kofi Awoonor Literary Prize. She spends her free time working with the Writers Project of Ghana, Flash Fiction Ghana and the Library of Africa and the African Diaspora. She holds a degree in English and Music from the University of Ghana. Elizabeth currently lives and works in Accra.

ESCAPED

Mariska Araba Taylor-Darko

It was a wet English summer's day. I had just got back home from the hospital. The usual story. He hit me, no not hit, but beat me… again. The other times that this happened, I covered my eyes with dark glasses when I went out. But this time, my contact lens got stuck to my eyeball and it was swollen. My cheeks were bruised and I had a blue black eye. I could not hide behind sunglasses. I ended up at the accident and emergency department.

We were a normal family like every other family I knew. Not perfect but then no family is perfect. We had friends from the same country and spoke the same language. Most of our friends worked and at weekends we got together with our children for barbecues and parties. Going out as a family full of smiles and happiness, shopping for the bring and share afternoons, buying gifts for friends celebrating birthdays or christenings for their new born babies were all normal family life. Nothing showed that things would turn out like this — that one day I would not want to go out because of a bruised face or black eyes.

I had left once before when things turned violent. It started when he began gambling heavily, and losing heavily. He had lost his job and I was now the breadwinner. It was then that he wanted to show me who had authority in our home. If he gave any money for housekeeping on a Friday, you could be sure that on a Saturday afternoon he would be demanding it back to bet on horse racing. I had to go grocery shopping by seven in the morning just to make sure something was in the house before those demands came. The demands came with punches and slaps and being blamed for the horses losing because of my bad luck.

When he brought other women into the house in my absence, under the guise of friendship, I knew I had had enough. When I found strange hairs on my pillow, I knew these visits were not just because of friendship; they were intimate relationships. I was accused of being jealous for nothing. I felt hurt that he could sleep with other women on our marital bed. Any query or attempt at getting answers was just me asking for trouble.

I moved out and stayed with a friend while I applied for an injunction to protect me from further abuse. I had also applied for and got legal separation. Due to the repetitive assaults nearly every other day, I was put on the waiting list for another flat for my son and I. Finally I was offered a two bedroom flat, it was one street away from my old house. It didn't feel safe but I accepted the offer. Moving a child from one school to another within the same Borough was a long drawn-out process with evaluations and other visits by social workers. These were things I did not want to go through. For now, my son could attend his school and have contact with his friends. He was my major concern.

I suffered mostly from fear those days. I would jump when I heard footsteps passing by my window in the night. I would be on the alert at the sound of a car parking outside the house. When I wasn't expecting a delivery or the social worker, my reaction to door knocks were always the same: I would jump up, my heart would pound with terror and my mouth would go dry. I hardly had a good night's sleep. At the least sound outside, I would wake up, lay rigid and still and silent in case he was in the house.

From nine to five on weekdays, I felt safe because I was at work, but on the bus home dread built up my stomach. Each bus stop closer to where I picked up my son was filled with apprehension. I would break out in sweat. My heart would pound and I would keep on glancing around and be on my guard. Would he be hanging around the area? Even with the injunction, nothing stopped him from being just outside the stipulated distance. I often saw him hanging around at the end of the road whenever I passed by. I felt he was stalking me.

I was having to endure handing our son over for weekend visits with him. After just two days with him, my son became aggressive, moody and sullen around the house. It was as though he was blaming me for something. It would take me a few days to get him back to being the same son I knew, cheerful, always asking questions and helpful around the house. These swings in his mood were events I feared would never end. It was a very unpleasant period in my life, having to go through the stress of worrying about my job, my son and, and the uncertainty of what tomorrow would bring. Being hurt by the person you once loved makes you realize some harsh truths. It taught me that trusting someone could be detrimental. It showed me the true colours of toxicity in people. It gave me lessons in life.

Flash forward. The ambulance driver who brought me home asked if I would be ok. I said yes I would be fine. I didn't really want to discuss my personal business with him. The shame and embarrassment of the situation made me keep my problems to myself. Before he left, he made sure I was going to be safe by asking me about the security in the house, whether I had changed the locks on the doors and whether I had someone to come and stay with me for a while. I looked up at this middle aged Englishman wondering why he wouldn't just leave.

"Young lady," he said, "Do you intend to be going through this all the time?" I shook my head and tears welled up in my eyes. "Look, nothing stops you from leaving this toxic relationship. You could move to another part of the country. You could leave this country. You should report to the Police. Make an effort to save yourself. Do you want your son to bury his mother? I have seen this many times before. Don't feel embarrassed if you have to ask for help. Sometimes you just can't handle a situation on your own." I had never thought about that. That fear of making any drastic decision, that fear of being followed wherever I would run to, that fear that I was as useless as I was being made to feel, was making me tolerate the intolerable. "Just think seriously about what I have said and save yourself." He gave me a list of numbers of various women support groups that he had in his notebook and left.

How could I do all the things that he had suggested? Was I strong enough to go through all this and come out unscathed? What would people think? I felt hopeless and desperate.

Being in such a situation made things go round and round in my mind. How would I manage? Where would I stay? Would he come after me? Would I be safe? The ache in my stomach was never ending.

In the UK, when you report to the police you are given the name of a legal aid centre and there you are given legal advice and assistance. You are guided through the process of applying for an injunction to keep your harasser away from you. These things take time. The Courts don't provide immediate action. You are not moved into a safe house immediately. You have to go through the process, but waiting for the process could get you killed. You have to take matters into your own hands if you want to survive.

The whole issue was so embarrassing I didn't know who to confide in. Friends that we both knew were divided in their loyalty. They always said I should have patience and that things would work out. After that conversation with a total stranger, someone who was not judgmental or partial to one side or another I felt a glimmer of hope. I decided to make a new life somewhere far away. I wanted to give my son a better future, to keep him away from a violent father and to break that behaviour from becoming the norm. He would not become a stereotype. I wanted him to grow into a black man who respected women, who had compassion and who was full of positivity.

Some months later I called a friend in Europe and asked if I could come over to stay with her for a short holiday. It would be a short break away from everything. She was so happy I called and when I told her all that had happened she asked why I didn't call her earlier. "Why don't you move here permanently?" she suggested in between weeping and laughing. I had an EU Passport so it was not going to be trouble relocating to another European country. She was a survivor too and a mother with a young son. Chatting to someone who had gone through the same abuse, and who was now at peace encouraged me to make that life-changing decision.

Finally I went on the holiday with my son. We had a great time in Denmark. We met friends of my friend, enjoyed good food, visited the famous Tivoli Gardens and sailed across to Sweden for the organised day trips on the hovercraft. Being summertime, there were many outdoor events. The days were longer than the nights so there was more opportunity to enjoy a full day. There was no looking over my shoulder every time I stepped out. I had a full night's sleep with no dreams and nightmares. My son was relaxed, not stressed out. I didn't realise how much the whole situation had affected him and when I asked him if he would like to stay in the new country, he didn't even hesitate to say yes.

Going back for the next few months was not something we looked forward to. The mandatory parental visits were no pleasure for him since he was just drilled and questioned about everything that happened in the house. Who came here? Where did you go? And all that. These are things that children should not be dragged into. Because of this, I didn't let my son know my plans. We were both dreaming about the holiday we had and I had to let it remain just a dream in case he was interrogated by his father. This thing of forcing a child to choose between parents and forcing a child to report on a parent caused my son distress. Slowly, arrangements fell into place for the big move. Having something to look forward to reduced some of the stress and anxiety because I knew that soon it would be over. Before making that move, there were legal things to take care of.

One day I made my journey out of the UK with my son. It wasn't until we were halfway across the ocean that I told him we were not coming back. I had packed all our clothes, my few favourite kitchen utensils, our books and most of all our important documents. Everything else was left behind.

I made my move to a new country, learnt a new language, and got a new job. It was not easy abandoning everything, but it was necessary. To assimilate into the new country and culture, we both went to language classes, which was compulsory. If you wanted a job, whether it was a cleaning job or higher, you had to learn the language. I remember asking my friend if a mop and bucket spoke Danish. After all, cleaning and mopping was universal. If you can work properly, you can work properly. This was on a lighter note. The tongue twisting exercises and homework kept me busy. They took my mind off the past. I made friends easily and soon had quite a few like-minded friends. It was through determination and resilience that things fell into place. Once my son made friends, after being accepted in a bilingual school, once he felt at peace and smiled each day, looking forward to the next new adventure as a tourist, I was also at peace. I acknowledged my self-worth. Sleep did not elude me. Actually I sometimes overslept. I was like the phoenix out of the ashes. Escaping was not such a bad thing after all.

Mariska Araba Taylor-Darko is a writer, poet and motivational speaker. She has published a motivational book, *The Secret to Detoxifying Your Life and Love*, a non-fiction book titled *The Deer Hunt*, and *The Iced Water Seller*, a fiction novel for young teens and is in the process of completing a children's full colour book titled *King Goat Aponkye* which will be a series. Her children's story "The Proud Peacock" was included in *Story Story Story Come*, an anthology of twelve winning stories in an international competition held in 2019. She has been featured in five poetry anthologies and two poems have been translated into Spanish.

Mariska is a member of the Ghana Association of Writers, the International Women's Writing Guild and WO2WA (West Africa 2 West Oakland) poetry group which has members from West Africa and the USA. She also has a blog page of her poetry on www.africanwomanspoetry.blogspot.com.

THE LONG-AWAITED ONE

Priscilla Adipa

I lost my arm in a zoo.

That's what Afriyie tells them when they stare with bewildered eyes and look away at the sight of her empty left sleeve which holds nothing but air. She looks out for the shock, almost invites it as her neighbours pass her in the courtyard, pretending not to look. Not ready to answer their questions, she keeps to herself, only coming out onto her balcony when the children from the surrounding apartments come out to play.

They come after school and on weekends, into the green courtyard around which five blocks of apartments stand in a horseshoe. They sit on the grass near the swings and slides. They chase one another around the trampoline until dizziness overcomes them. They dress up their dolls or throw a ball around until their mothers and older sisters call them back in. The obedient ones go quietly, but some groan, say, "I'm coming," and only move when their mothers return, wagging a finger.

Lately, Afriyie's trips onto her balcony have become focused on a little boy. He showed up on the balcony of the topmost apartment in the next block on a day the rain kept the children inside. He watched her as she drifted in and out of sleep on her lounge chair, his face appearing and disappearing as she opened and closed her eyes, so it was as though they were playing hide and seek. Intrigued, Afriyie stopped napping to gaze at the boy's face, inserted between the squares of the guardrails.

He waved. Tentatively at first, then more vigorously when her eyes didn't leave his. She wanted to say something, but the words remained trapped in the back of her throat. She took too long. He waved again and scurried back inside.

One afternoon, Afriyie leaves her balcony to sit under the jacaranda trees in the courtyard, where four metallic benches have been arranged in a single line. She watches the little boy and his friends playing football in the middle of the courtyard.

"Shoot!"

"Pass!"

"Goal!"

The wind carries their shouts over. It's as though she's a part of their game. Sure enough, the ball shoots through the air towards her. She stands to pick it up as the little boy runs to her. She hands it to him. "Who's winning?" she asks.

"My team," he shouts as he dashes back to his friends.

Afriyie studies him in awe, her energetic little miracle, kicking with short, stubby legs, waving his arms in the air when the ball enters the short goalpost on the far side, close to the swings and slides. She sucks in her breath when he falls; almost rushes to him when he doesn't get up fast enough.

She stays in the courtyard long after the children leave, wondering how she would manage if she had one of her own.

Back in her apartment, she takes out the box of baby clothes from the wardrobe in the second bedroom. Onesies, tops, bibs. Neutral colours because she hadn't wanted to know the sex of the baby.

It was a boy. A boy who had stopped breathing after he was pulled from her. A boy fully formed with ten tiny fingers and ten toes. How could he stop breathing when he was so well formed?

A month after the burial she had told her mother, who had come from Mthatha to Johannesburg a week before her due date, to pack the baby clothes into the box. A few days after, she panicked when she found her mother in her bedroom doing just that.

"What are you doing?" she shouted, before snatching the romper from her mother's hand.

Tears clouding her eyes, she dragged the box into the corridor, past the kitchen, then the living room. She moved towards the front door, her face firm, so her mother stood back and said nothing. But keys in hand, door ajar, security gate still locked, she stopped. She couldn't throw the box away. He never wore the clothes, but she couldn't help seeing traces of the baby's soul in them – little bits of a person, the smells, the fingerprints we stamp on our belongings and leave behind when we die.

She had selected each item of clothing carefully, imagining little arms in sleeves, little feet in socks. Her due date pending, she had washed them to remove the touch of factory hands.

Now, she pulls the box into her room, where the baby's cot still sits next to her bed. Slowly, she folds the clothes into neat little shapes and arranges them on an empty shelf in her wardrobe.

Afriyie smiles more often. Particularly when she sees the little boy. She enjoys the children's laughter around her, as he becomes the constant in her new routine. One afternoon, she takes her eyes off him once, twice, and when she looks again, he is gone from the courtyard. She doesn't see him the next day or the day after. She decides to search for him.

She doesn't know what she'll say to his parents when she arrives at their apartment. She simply allows her anxiety to push her up the stairs to the third floor. She reaches the stairs below their apartment, and it is here that the force behind her gives way to fear. She stops. She steps forward but misses a step. She bends over. Her phantom left hand reaches out for the cream-coloured wall. She steadies herself for a second. She falls.

On her way back to her apartment, Afriyie considers the absence on the left side of her body; the things it prevents her from doing. She can no longer care for a baby without help. She would struggle to change and bathe one. Yet she still wants a child.

Days go by without her seeing the little boy, and darkness overwhelms her. She hides under a blanket and ignores the clouded view of the Johannesburg skyline from her bedroom window. She does not see the jagged lightning that saws the skyline in half – on one side, the high-rises in the city centre; on the other, the yellow ash of the Soweto mine dumps.

He returns after seven days. From a trip outside of Jo'burg, it seems. Through her bedroom window she watches them in the parking lot below. Father removing suitcases from the boot; the little boy helping his little sister with their toys; Mother directing it all.

Bile rises in her throat. She runs to the bathroom and releases nothing from her empty stomach. All the same, Afriyie sees vomit in the toilet bowl, dregs of the healthy breakfasts she made for herself during her pregnancy.

She turned to IVF after a third round of artificial insemination proved unsuccessful. "Probably due to age," her doctor had said, as he reminded her of the varying success rates of differently aged women – the science of the body that was unresponsive to her prayers. His reasoning only spurred her on. Once again, she selected a sperm donor from a range of profiles: tall, short, black, white, Indian, coloured. The invented family. She imagined men jerking off in little rooms, their eyes trained on glossy images of naked women. The romance of making a family.

For more than a week she injected herself with hormones so her body would produce extra eggs. She checked in with her doctor every other day. On her fourth visit, she heard him say she had made good progress. It was time for her eggs to be harvested.

She gave a curt nod and retreated further into herself, to stay detached from the hope buried deep inside her stomach. She gazed at the potted plants on the filing cabinet in the corner of the doctor's office, then at the collage of photos on the wall behind the doctor – photos of women and a few men, beaming with smiles, cradling babies with plump cheeks. She stared at the doctor's bald head, bent over her file. He scribbled in busy cursive writing she couldn't decipher. He raised his head when he was done and asked in his usual brisk tone, "So, can you do tomorrow or the day after?"

She scanned her calendar in her mind's eye. A couple of staff meetings she could skip. She told him to book her in immediately.

At work the day after the harvesting, she hid in a small conference room to avoid the mindless chatter of her colleagues. She tried to catch up on work, but all she could do was look blankly at the documents populating her computer screen. She marvelled that in a hospital not far away, the sperms of a faceless man were latching onto her eggs, piercing them to form life. She felt cheated. A petri dish was doing what her body would not – bringing the crucial ingredients together, forming a living thing.

The doctor transferred three embryos into her uterus in line with her wishes. She felt a new weight in her womb, and although he had told her she could go to work, she spent a week in bed, her legs propped up on pillows to keep the embryos inside.

She made plans while she waited, even as she tried not to. She would move her desk to the second bedroom, place a chest of drawers for the baby's clothes in the corner where the desk was. The cot could go next to her bed and she would buy a rocking chair for night-time feeds. Afriyie closed her eyes and prayed.

She was rewarded. Her pregnancy test came up positive.

She heard nothing else after the news. She was floating above ground, embracing the months ahead, the check-ups, the thrill of seeing her stomach swell up, the swollen ankles, the planning. She felt complete.

She waited four months before telling Frema, her sister. On a Skype call to the US, Afriyie lifted her body from the sofa to show off her bump. Pride stretched the sides of her mouth as Frema ululated. For once, Frema's theatrics didn't bother Afriyie. She turned from side to side like a model, soaking in the attention.

Frema said, "So, how are you? I hope your morning sickness is over. When I had Aseda, it continued into my fifth month. Can you imagine? With Yaw it was better. Maybe because Aseda was the first. You'll see. They grow so fast, and start walking and talking and doing all sorts of things. I mean look at Aseda, already telling me what she'll wear and not wear!"

Afriyie was happy to sit there, hands cradling her stomach as Frema carried on about her children's exploits and how well her husband's medical practice was doing. On the computer screen, she watched Frema stick her head into a massive fridge and walk out of the frame holding a can of tomato puree. She heard drawers pulled open and the rush of water from a tap. Then, the clink of metal against glass and the sizzle of food being fried.

"I'm making jollof," Frema said. Then, "Have you told Mom?"

Afriyie hesitated, "Not yet."

"You know she can help."

"I'll be fine."

"Trust you to say that. How will you cope?"

It was a question her mother would ask too.

"I mean, Patrick can be useless sometimes, but at least he can occupy the kids when my hands are full. I'm telling you, it's not easy ohh! It helps to have another pair of hands, even if it's a man's."

Frema's words felt like a jab. Afriyie narrowed her eyes and said, "Well, I don't have a choice. I'll make do."

"Really?" Frema said, "I really don't understand you, Afriyie! You could have had any of them. I mean, Kwame would have done anything for you, and you let that Sena have him. And Steve? You guys even lived together!" Frema went on in a frustrated tone, as though she was the one whom Steve had left.

Afriyie stopped listening. Frema's words drove deep into incisions she thought had healed, drawing fresh blood. It was because she still asked herself the same questions.

"I'm just saying," Frema concluded, "You were so popular at Wits. What happened?"

Afriyie shrugged.

With Frema in the US and her mother all the way in Mthatha in the Eastern Cape, Afriyie attended antenatal classes alone, or sometimes with friends. She forced herself to ignore the smug looks from pregnant wives, and instead focused on being the good student she'd always been during sessions on how to breathe during labour, and how to hold and breastfeed a newborn.

Eventually, she called her mother in Mthatha.

"I guess we live in a different world now," her mother said, "These days, it's easier to do what you are doing." After a long silence, she added, "I wonder what your father would have thought about all this." Which was her mother's way of saying she thought something about all this but wouldn't say it.

Whatever she thought, her mother was with her in the delivery room, offering her hand to be squeezed when contractions consumed her. And, after the emergency C-section, she was the one to tell her, with pain in her eyes, that there was no child to hold. Only the phrase "complications during surgery," weighing on the raw skin of Afriyie's person.

Mpho. Gift.

A Sotho word not in her vocabulary, but one that makes sense the afternoon after his return, when a ball rolls to Afriyie's feet and she picks it up for the little boy running towards her.

"Thank you," he says as he turns to run off.

Afriyie stops him, "And what is your name?"

"Mpho."

"Mpho. What a lovely name."

"It means gift." He offers this information because he has heard his mother say, "Mpho, my gift." Then he asks, pointing at the emptiness on the left side of her body, "What happened?"

She has been ready for the question for some time now.

"I had an accident when I went to the hospital," she says, thinking about the intravenous drip that gave her the infection after the C-section.

"And the doctor couldn't fix you?"

"Unfortunately, no."

"Sorry," he says.

She smiles in response as he runs off. She wants to call him back, but she lets him go.

Priscilla Adipa is a Ghanaian writer and Assistant Professor in the Humanities and Social Sciences at the International University of Grand-Bassam in Côte d'Ivoire. Her short stories, which explore questions related to grief, identity, desire, and family dynamics, have appeared in Transition, Obsidian: Literature & Arts in the African Diaspora, *Kenkey for Ewes and Other Very Short Stories* and Brittle Paper. Through her work, Priscilla delves into the lives of people living not only in Ghana, but also in South Africa and Côte d'Ivoire. A sociologist trained at Northwestern University in the US, she is interested in how individuals are shaped by their relationships and the places they find themselves in. Her research on the ways in which exhibition openings and talks with artists influence arts participation and the evaluation and interpretation of art has been published in Poetics. Born and raised in Accra, Priscilla currently lives in Abidjan.

SELF SEARCH

Nana Frema Busia

I looked at the strange person in the mirror. Recognition eluded me. Who is this person living inside of me, invading me. I do not know this stranger, this usurped device, a pretext? A misnomer in my name living in me.

What is this guessing game in a void shell, this chance encounter overwhelming my existence!

But I must adapt, I must meet myself, integrate the reality and reject the falsehood, search for myself within the deep crevices of spoilage, the ruins, the encountered diabolical constructs that have me lost within myself and surrender to truths that are fool proof.

I must yield to a new self
Derive an awareness with an assurance devoid of false labels.
I must reach out and hold on to God's treasuries of pleasantries.

Kokrokoo, ade akye!
I cannot mourn the morning
I must Yield to worthy Evocations that shield what is right
I must Revel in emersions of light with Godly might
I must Overcome blankets of smoke that predict night
And Conquer by beaming rays of sunny smiles that are bright

I must Kick the darkness goodbye from the sky
I must Rekindle hugs of love
from above
And Kiss the music of life
while alive.
I must, I must,
I shall.

BECOMING

Nana Frema Busia

Listening
Intently
Trying to hear my own rhythm
Irregular heartbeat
Pomp depomp pomp

Am I moving steadfast
OR standing stagnant
Will God speak
OR has he already spoken

Where is the pivotal direction
What are the next steps

Shall I go with my own flow which misdirected the path to the non-place which engulfed the tears and fused it with bright stars in a gloomy float?

Do I wait in weariness for the sound that will herald and profess greatness with a hidden glow?

Where is that place without shame that does not wear pain
Show me the lane that promises that panacea without disdain
Show me the never ending rotation
that revolves in laughter reflective and golden

For I am laden with uncertainty and a fleeting scene of silent foreboding

I have forgiven all nightmares that impact the restless journey

How do I defy conflicting overtures to arrive at new exhilarating memories

Do I shrug at the past and head to unknown charters of discovery in recovery

Do I wallow in a pool of stoic confinement that is solitary in blissful solemnity

Do I reach out to a mischievous dangling earth glittering like a solitaire
When there is a heavenly street
paved with diamonds at my
Feet
Heralding no defeat?
How do I the risen Christ receive
And the herald of goodness achieve?

Becoming

How do I overcome "my-self"
And become my spirit sense

If my ingrained nature is a den of sin
How do I dim the flawed crescendo
To transcend the flesh
To live afresh

Help me in my gory imperfections
Enroll me in the promised spirit body
For reliance on your reflective Glory

Listening aright
Intently again
Absorbing the light

It is not a game
To regain life.

Nana Frema Busia is a California attorney at law and a writer. She currently lives in Accra, Ghana.

KUBOLOR COUNTRY

Ekow Manuar

Sun de come! I for gedup. But my body de itch. How I for do? Sammy no de? Oh my goodness gracious yesu cristo – my body de itch! Like I for bath or something. I for go my parent in der. See if some money de wait me. Mommy go like see me sef... But Poppy? Chale... Sun de come out. Aish, chale, what I for do?

These are the thoughts of a man – well, a boy, at the tail end of a drug binge that has seen him gallivant the streets through the night from Osu to Pig Farm, looking to score any sort of a high. This boy is Kwamena, and it is the early hours of a Tuesday morning, 16th March, 2029. However, it is of no consequence which date Kwamena wakes to. The way this day unfolds is similar to each one since he left his parents' home and took up with Sammy's crew.

Sammy's crew offered Kwamena something of a rope to a life of acceptance, at the very least; and fraternity, of which he had been quite deprived in the cramped compound of his family's household. Kwamena would sometimes reminisce about the life he'd had under his family's rusting roofing sheets. Nights spent on his backside with his hands tight by his sides to squeeze in with his sweaty older brothers. Musty armpits mixed with footballing feet. Mornings marching to the water stations to fetch and carry water back in time for his father's breakfast. Sneers following him with accusations of being effeminate. From street boys. But mostly from his own brothers. Then, afternoons spent with his mother at the marketplace. Loving at times. Stern when times were rough.

Yes, that was his old life and he wanted nothing more to do with it. But even he would admit – when he was sober enough to – that this new life came with one too many caveats.

Just the previous night, he, Sammy and Tiwa had ambushed a car at a traffic light. Tiwa, an on-and-off member of the crew, had approached the car pretending to wipe the windscreen, and while the driver shooed her away, Kwamena had smashed the passenger window with a rock. Sammy followed hot on his tail in an attempt to force themselves into the passenger seat. Obviously, this was all done under the influence of a toxic combination of Tramadol and codeine stirred together in a pot, a concoction that made them more drowsy than any car-jacker needed to be. Needless to say, their target sped off in a cloud of dust and screeching tires.

Afterwards, Sammy and Kwamena went their own way. They first went back to scratch and sniff up the residue of their earlier concoction, then they hit the dimly-lit streets of Old Accra to continue the hunt for money or drugs. Unfortunately for the two, they ended up falling asleep instead.

And this is where we find our protagonist, Kwamena, waking up from an anxious sleep amid fifteen other lost souls spread out on the pavement in front of a KFC.

If I find Sammy, we can go to our spot and do some trama. Then, I go go to Mommy? But Sammy sef, how I go find am? Phone? Ha! Sometimes my head de mash-up. My phone dey plus Sammy! Then I for go Mommy? Ah, Sammy too! Like if we go the spot then cha, my head go make clear. Oooooh. I no wan go Mommy in place. Ah, but – but – make I ask this person for the time. If it knack 7, then Mommy go de the shop. Aish, but the shop, e far, or? Ewarade nyacopon! Wat dis matta?

The time was 10.34 am, almost four hours since Kwamena had woken up. He had spent a good two hours searching for a bathroom to relieve himself in. However, he was so distracted by a series of episodes brought on by his flaring drug withdrawals that he almost forgot about his colonic issues. Shivering, sweating and smelling worse than his brother's armpits, Kwamena resolved to hold on to his bottom, remembering that his primary destination was his mother's tomato stall in Agbogbloshie.

He tried to get a trotro – surprisingly, he had enough credit for it – but the driver's mate refused to let him in.

"My friend, you de mell! You shank yourself? You no for step here, kraa!" The mate marked an imaginary line in front of the trotro stop, "Dis be registered trotro, e no be public toilet!"

"O mami, wai! Why, your trotro be made of gold? See ur face, like you no go get my shank sef... Sia!"

And before the mate could react, Kwamena was scampering off in the opposite direction, scratching and glancing nervously over his shoulder. Once walking, he decided it was his best mode of transportation.

The sun was wrecking Kwamena as he trudged on beneath its fire. He had lost his way, only to be redirected by some plastic scavengers who chased him away from a pile of trash he was set to ease himself in. It was after they threw their chalewote at him and signaled in the direction of the Agbogboloshie e-waste dumpsite (Go where you belong!) that he rerouted and marched onwards. But that had been hours ago.

Stupid boy! How you no know that the place be far like dat? Chale, my head de mash up! Maybe I for relax on the tramadol small. Cos dis one dierrr, ah! Like I walk my whole life, dis. Goat sef no de walk like dis. But, at least, when I see Mommy she go give something make I chop, gather my energy small. Then, off to Sammy. I go fi use Mommy phone call my phone and see where he dey.

Finally, Kwamena turned onto the road leading to Agbogbloshie. He could see the columns of smoke rising from the infamous dumpsite. The market came into view – a jumble of people, animals, cars, trucks, bicycles and carts crisscrossing each other like some gigantic ant parade. But, just as with ants, this jumbled mess was actually a functional ecosystem, permeated with smells from foul to fresh, and with sounds of varying frequencies. Women advertising their wares, chickens clucking, policemen harassing, and the tired wheels of barrels rolling along the filth-laden ground. Then there was the heightened awareness that such a cacophony brings – that, at any moment you're going to get trodden on or run into…

As Kwamena staggered between people and animals, digital boards and cleaning stations, the way to his mother's stall slowly came back to him. The itching and shakes had grown worse, but our little hero was grounded by his mission of getting his mother's phone so that he could call his own, which was on Sammy, and Sammy was where the drugs were. If only he could find Sammy, he could clear his head and then – yes – then, he would start the tramadol detox. Tramadol was no good for him, he had decided, because… well, because he had just walked across Old Accra like a Fulani's goat, and that was not what he intended his life to be.

His mother's stall was easy to spot. It had the largest MTN umbrella of any tomato seller within the inner part of the market.

Kwamena approached the stall and saw his mother bending down to gather tomatoes for a waiting customer. When she got up, he ran over and hugged her from behind.

"Ah, who is that?" She turned around to face Kwamena, "FOOLISH TWAT! WHAT IT IS THE MEANING OF THIS? GET OFF MY BOTTOM BEFORE I BEAT YOU UP!"

It wasn't his mother. It was Maame Augusta, another tomato seller. Augusta forgot about her customer and reached for a slipper to slap Kwamena, who was motoring backwards.

Before she could reach him, his actual mother appeared, begging Augusta to spare her son.

"Sister Augusta, forgive his stupidity! He got it from me! Please…"

"He's high again, isn't he? How could he do such a thing? No correct person would…"

"Exactly Augusta! You have said it yourself – he is not correct."

"He never was! You see, I told you – you shouldn't have let him do women's work in the house!" Augusta calmed down and turned back to her waiting customer.

"My son, what is all this?" Kwamena's mother beat off filth from her boy's clothes before holding him at arm's length to take him in fully. They had moved away from the chaos and were now under the shade of her MTN umbrella.

"Mommy, please I wan use your phone."

"To do what?"

"To call my phone."

"Why, where is it?"

Kwamena looked away and scratched under his neck.

"Why don't you come home? Take a shower, eat and rest, okay?"

"Oh, Mommy! Like, that is my plan too! I want to come home."

"Then let's go." She pulled him along.

"No!" Kwamena resisted, "I need to call my phone!"

"Why?"

"Like, if I call my phone, then I go know where Sammy de. Then I go fi clear my head. Then de itching go stop. Then I go fi come home to you, Mommy. I wan get better…"

"Good! Then let's go!" She tried again but he resisted, more fiercely this time.

"No! I NEED to call my phone!" Kwamena tried to wriggle out of his mother's grasp. He thrashed this way and that, but she held firm. Suddenly, he was hollow inside and couldn't stand upright anymore. The emptiness seemed to have spread to the very limits of him, as if it would only take a breeze to carry him off to the netherworld. "I beg, Mommy, please! Make I call my phone…"

But his mother wouldn't let go of him now that he was in her clutches. Maybe there was no hope for him. Maybe there was no hope for anyone. It didn't stop one trying and it wouldn't stop her. For her son. Even if her husband insulted her for it. Even if the pastor had dared sack her from church. They were hopeless cases in their own right as far as she was concerned. Kwamena, her last son of five, deserved better than to be another kubolor on the streets of Accra.

Ekow Manuar is the up and coming African Futurist writer of our time. Hailing from Accra, Ghana, and educated as a Sustainability Scientist in Europe, Ekow Manuar is more than a writer. He co-founded and runs an agribusiness company that grows vegetables and fruits for the local market. He has developed and financed renewable energy projects for residential, commercial, and industrial customers.

After work hours, Ekow Manuar contemplates the futures of West Africa and this is reflected in his work. He has published his stories in the Lund UPF Magazine in Sweden, in the UK with the Dark Mountain publication, with the online literary Nigerian magazine Mbari and a Pan African online magazine Kalahari Review. His published works include 'A Prayer on the Train,' 'The Days Before the World Ended,' 'The Stories We Tell,' and 'Tell Me What You See.' You can see his other work on his medium (https://abdallahsmith06.medium.com/).

FAFANTO

Akua Serwaa Amankwah

Everything shifted the day Eno chanced upon her seven year-old self in her old neighbourhood, the decadent Ridge with its verdant trees. Of course, anyone seeing their mini-me twenty-one years later would have gasped in fright, or prayed it a dream. But it was not a dream, and Eno was too intrigued, too filled with wonder and a dull emotion she couldn't describe, to wish it an illusion. She had seen many of her younger selves before, but they were always blurred, meaningless blobs of strangers, stuck in different times. This was something else. The young One was right here, in the flesh.

She was back in the affluent Ridge Estates, filled with neighbours who lived large; exporters of cocoa, merchants and market queens of Makola, owners of gigantic warehouses and businesses from tiles to tyres. Her family had no such background. They had moved here thanks to Daa's 'smart money decision.' It was 1996, and people burned by the Pyram scam now kept their money at home and viewed banks with scepticism and disdain. Daa had signed up for it early and brought the striped green and white forms home. That was how they had bought the semi-finished home in Ridge and completed it. When church members came, he joined them in prayers of torture for the Pyram directors, leaving out that he had enjoyed his share of interest.

Everything seemed scaled down now. The childhood home that had been a mansion to her looked like an average two-storey. A sleek black Peugeot crawled up the driveway next door and a family in resplendent kente came out, chattering excitedly. In other driveways kids were laughing, riding bicycles, jumping rope, girls shrieking over a game of *tumatu*. She watched, mulling over the carefreeness of childhood. She had not been carefree.

Shoulders slumped, the young One glanced uncertainly back at the house before slipping money into the back pocket of her jeans. She had been sent on an errand. Eno stared back at the house, spotless with a fresh coat of cream paint, surrounded by manicured lawns so perfect they seemed artificial.

Eno followed the young One down the familiar pathway at a safe distance, wondering what would happen if she turned and faced her. What would you tell your young self once you had most of the answers? Would you douse everything in sugar or serve the truth – a mirror of life with its uncertainties and surprises, nasty and delightful? The child rubbed at her backside and Eno knew at once that Daa had beaten her up again; one of his signature whippings with his belt. She winced because, for a moment, she was in sync with the child, feeling the welts – soft, uneven reminders of familiar, stinging pain.

The girl dawdled for a while before stopping at Tiptoe Store and Eno knew she was stalling. Even a few extra minutes away from home were precious. Both hesitated when they got back to the familiar grey gates. Everyone seemed to see through Eno so she was safe, yet when she reached the entrance, she stopped short.

Home. The intricate wooden door leading to misery. Beyond it, framed photographs – the perfect family unit, frozen in time in their posed smiles. Daa – strict, bespectacled, with a temper that knew no bounds; Mamaa, the eternal pleaser; Nipaa, the sibling par excellence; Naasei, the drug supplier connoisseur, and, well, Eno.

There were vintage glass and wooden sideboards teeming with plates, glasses and mugs; a melee of meaningless purchases, gifts and wedding souvenirs. She remembered the contents of the three drawers in the middle without having to open them. Christmas cards in the first – from academics and fervent worshippers at Daa's church: Prof. and Elaine Kwawukume; the overbearing Lutterodts whose extravagant Christmas gifts gave them the right to call Daa for prayers at ungodly hours; the Sarpongs who would visit with groceries enough for an army, complete with a white envelope heavy with fresh notes; the Bannermans whose son Ebow had chased Nipaa for so long that Eno wanted to tell the poor boy yes on her rigid sister's behalf.

Obituaries filled the second drawer, and the third was reserved for school reports and certificates from all three of them, from straight A's to "What is this mess of a grade?" That dent on the left of the drawer – the day Naasei smoked himself into a high that made him destroy everything and threaten anyone who came close.

The hall. This was where Pastor Halm had sat with Daa, racked with sobs the day his daughter Efe died in a hit-and-run. For months, whenever she was on errands, the young One dreamed a car would graze her bottom and she would be thrown up in the air in dramatic slow motion and return peacefully to the earth with a thud, not breathing. She would lie in the street, eyes open, with the blank, surprised look of the dead in movies, but then, she would resurrect. Daa would regret ever laying his hands on her, and actually apologise. Maa would dote on her and make her sandwiches with freshly baked bread slathered with Planta margarine and a chilled Refresh juice box on the side. Naasei would be nice to her, and Nipaa would stop acting like she didn't exist.

The kitchen. Where Daa slapped Naasei because he had brought a girl into his room. Naasei fought back, and it would have ended terribly had Mamaa not intervened. If there was one thing he had inherited from Daa, it was that fiery temper, only new, improved and more lethal.

Eno stood dazed till she realised things were changing. The young One was ten now. She had gained weight, eating to submerge the pain, the fights, the screams, the whippings. The whippings! Administered like Vitamins: Vitamin You Failed in Maths, Vitamin You Shouldn't Have Talked Back, Vitamin You're a Church Elder's Daughter.

This was the year she had got a penpal through a class exchange organised by her favourite teacher, Miss Elma Lartey. She was paired with the delightful Halle Adjeman from New York. Halle told her everything. Their letters were heavy with family secrets and tales from school, and any money the young One got disappeared into envelopes and stamps. She couldn't wait for the next letter. Halle told her about her dreams to become a doctor, her twin sisters who were so beautiful she felt like a blot beside them, her uncle who had locked himself up in his room because his favourite girlfriend had left him. The young One, in turn, told Halle how she wished she could escape the beatings and sleep in a sea of stars, drinking one glass after another of *fula* with milk and groundnuts; how she wanted to talk and laugh with her siblings; how she'd overheard her parents' conversation and suspected that Mamaa had once wronged Daa and he had still not forgiven her.

Then, she was caught copying during exams. A church elder's daughter, a cheat! Daa hurled prayers at her as he whipped her, as if the fire and the burning would enter her and weed out 'that stubbornness.' He asked her headmistress to be harsher in her punishment so that everyone would know what she had done. The seniors had a field day picking on her, making her kneel down, sweep and weed. Daa ransacked her room, and, when he found her letters with Halle, tore them up and forbade her to write to anyone. She tried to reach out to Nipaa, but she was too busy being the trophy daughter.

Nipaa, Nipaa, Nipaa. The scenery shifted to the compound where her sister had last been seen. 21st of December, 2000. One minute she was there, the next, she was off to buy something and never returned. Missing, that's how they reported it. *Missing.*

It was an infuriating word. A blurred line between giving up and moving on, like having your heart wrenched from your body and replaced with cotton wool or some such nonsense to fill in till the heart came back. But Nipaa never returned. She had been the glue that held the family together and now, it all came apart. Daa stayed out more often, and no one ate at the dining table anymore. Naasei, who had started university, stayed there over the vacations. Everyone was lost in their own world.

There were many theories about the disappearance of Nipaa – she had been kidnapped and killed, robbed and beaten, trafficked somewhere, had run away. The latter was what her parents insisted – Nipaa had run away. It was the nonchalance of the police that sent chills down her spine; how they wouldn't budge till you acted; how they behaved as if the only possible explanation for a young girl's disappearance was a visit to a boyfriend.

Eno accompanied the young One to Nipaa's room, marvelling as she stood at the entrance. Other than a film of dust that had settled over everything, nothing had changed. Her bed was laid with pale pink sheets bordered with red roses. On her night table was the beaded lamp which had stopped working a few months after being bought but was too beautiful to throw away. Stacks of books from Ama Ata Aidoo to Ahmadou Kourouma: Nipaa had studied Literature and French. Papers and receipts were stacked neatly on her desk. So typical of her. Eno felt herself shrouded by a familiar sadness and barely noticed that she'd been propelled four years forward.

Their house at Ridge had been sold; the family scattered. It started with Daa's affair with that lady whose breasts super-jiggled whenever she came up to greet him at church – for other church members they merely jiggled. Her name was Abena Rose, and she always hovered around Daa at church, touching his elbow, breasts in his face. She came to him for prayers, for Bible interpretation. When Mamaa went to church camp, her visits became regular and she'd bring along banana bread, fish stew, groundnut soup, as if their fridge was empty.

"She's just a friend," Daa would insist when Mamaa came back.

"She's a tick!" Mamaa would scream.

"Are you saying I'm a dog?"

A new fight would break out. There were days when the young One was tempted to tell Daa just to leave her mother alone and continue his adultery in peace. She watched her parents' marriage disintegrate and something died inside her.

The afternoon Mamaa left, the young One felt it in her bones. She knew because her mother laughed for the first time in a long while. She made them her specialty – nuhuu studded with tuna and smoked crayfish, with a hint of ateagyaa leaves. Daa went for seconds, and despite their flash of affection for each other, the young One was suspicious. Mamaa didn't call Daa names. She didn't mock him for being an elder of Abena Rose's breasts. It was unsettling. Later that afternoon she went out on an errand and they did not see her again till months later, on a *Greetings from Abroad* TV programme, with a well-built man at her side. She sent good wishes and love to family back home as if everything was normal.

That day, Daa drank himself into oblivion. He later returned Mamaa's drinks to her family, sputtering invectives and ill-wishes to the elders. They insulted him back. Next they heard, he'd married Abena Rose and she had twin daughters whom he discovered weren't his on their fifth birthday.

The young One mourned. Mamaa had let go of her hand when she needed her most. She would be moved from home to home, enduring one form of abuse or another until she was deposited at her maternal grandmother's at seventeen.

The time shifts sped up, as if hurrying through Eno's life. The young One walked around blindly, counting the days when she too would start university and stay there, like Naasei. But she kept failing in school and had to take extra classes. After three tortuous years, she finally got in. Eno looked on as her young self began dancing in her newfound freedom. But she was still plagued with low grades. Nothing seemed to stick in her mind, and studying was tough.

Then she met AJ Appiah who knew how to hack the system, and life too, it seemed. She was introduced to The Circle, versed in the art of fraud – visa fraud, account takeovers, blackmailing influential people, posing as estate agents selling off non-existent houses, and – her favourite – identity theft. The thrill lay in being a different person for each act. No longer Eno with her ninety-nine problems. She was a god, crafting perfect women with dreamed-up names in between battling with her studies, adding bits of truths here and there to make them authentic, watching people fall for their wiles.

Things moved on smoothly until a man they had defrauded traced their activities and had them arrested. It was not until they were in the middle of police procedures that Eno realised this was the younger brother of Prof. Kwawukume, Daa's old friend and a sender of their 90s holiday cards. The Kwawukumes singled her out for questioning. They wanted to understand why things had turned out as they had for her. They probed and prodded and she uttered not a word. Once she unravelled one stitch, she would have to go all the way, and she couldn't bear to do that. But they stayed on her case, eventually giving her a choice between a psychiatrist and jail.

It was like asking a butterfly about her caterpillar days. Who wanted to remember those beginnings? She was a *fafanto* now, a butterfly; it was the beauty that blinded people and made them believe her. She would not, could not go back. She was ready to choose jail.

Then came the morning she was told she had a visitor. When the door opened and the woman peeped in, Eno held on to her seat, shaking. That heart shaped face with a sharp jaw; that impish, knowing smile and nappy hair which refused to grow, even in adulthood. She had never seen her, but they had exchanged photos. Halle Adjeman! Halle who knew the land of Eno's childhood like the back of her hand; now a psychiatrist.

"I've been looking for you for years," Halle said. They hugged, both crying, and Eno felt a strange sense of peace.

Halle didn't add that it was Miss Lartey who had contacted her on Facebook after reading about Eno's arrest in the papers, and had put her in touch with the Kwawukumes.

The morning Halle asked Eno to go back in time, Eno refused. She knew it meant going back to the whips and the welts; a journey back to torture.

"I don't remember," she said at first, but it was fruitless to lie to someone who knew.

"Eno, you do. Let's start…" Halle paused, "Let's start from the truth."

Tears burned in Eno's eyes and she looked away.

"Let's start from No. 6 Mango Road at Ridge. Your earliest memory."

On any other day, Eno would have found the perfect character to disappear into, but now, even she was curious. She closed her eyes and went back to a self that had witnessed not only her own abuse, but Nipaa, suspended from that tree with a rope, body limp and dangling; perfection made imperfect. Nipaa, finally free of her own demons. Her parents had covered up. Nipaa's escape was the beginning of Eno's entrapment and Naasei's nonchalance, and when Mamaa couldn't take it anymore, she had left. Each had chosen their refuge.

So, the morning Eno met her seven-year old self, she knew it would be difficult, but she had been looking for her for a while. She was going home, to where it all began.

Akua Serwaa Amankwah is a writer and an MPhil student specialising in Literature at the University of Ghana, Legon, with Creative Writing, African

Literature and Photography as her research interests. When Akua isn't lost in research, reading or writing, she is most likely exploring MasterClass sessions or putting together activity boxes for aesop studios, her children's subscription business.

She is currently working on a Young Adult novel and a collection of short stories.

COVID-19 AND THE ARTISTIC RESILIENCE

Wale Okediran

THE "NEW NORMAL"

The global health crisis arising from the COVID-19 pandemic and its corollaries of poverty, unfriendly policies and, in some instances, political upheavals have had a profound effect on arts and cultural heritage. The situation has complicated the conditions of livelihood for many artists, both employed and independent, across the sector. In adapting to the situation, artists just like other citizens have had to adjust to what has come to be known as the "New Normal".

The "New Normal" is not a new terminology. The term was used to describe the financial crisis of 2007-2008 and the aftermath of the 2008–2012 global recession. It describes a state that differs from the prevailing situation prior to the start of the crisis. This current "new normal" includes limiting person-to-person contact like handshakes and hugs. As long as the world has not found a cure or a vaccine for Covid-19, we may have to adjust to this "new normal". This requires a reimagining of new ways of living, working and interacting with people.

CLOSURES AND CANCELLATIONS

Through the first quarter of 2020, arts and culture sector organizations around the world progressively restricted their public activities and some closed completely due to the pandemic. By late March, most cultural heritage organizations had closed, and arts events were postponed or cancelled, either voluntarily or by government mandate. In-person exhibitions, events, and performances were cancelled or postponed. This affected galleries, libraries, archives, and museums (collectively known as GLAMs), as well as film and television productions, theatre and orchestra performances, concert tours, zoos, and music and arts festivals. Major commercial art fairs were also cancelled.

MAKING A LIVING AS AN ARTIST

Many authors support their income with public appearances, for example, as at festivals. They may also engage in professional activity in addition to writing, with such jobs typically being in teaching, research or journalism.

In their report "Creating a Living: Challenges for authors' Income," the International Author's Forum indicate that in some European countries and in the USA, about half of all authors made their incomes from writing alone. Apart from making multiple public appearances each year, authors generate income from primary sales of their original physical and digital content, secondary exploitations of such content including uses under licence, public lending right (PLR) payments, resale rights royalties, awards and grants.

Although there are presently no adequate figures from Africa, private communications suggest that less than 5% of African authors derived their incomes from writing work alone.

EFFECTS AND ADAPTATIONS TO THE UNFOLDING WORLD
Literature and publishing

As a result of the restrictions on gatherings, many literary festivals, commercial book fairs and book launches were cancelled or postponed. Many bookshops were also forced to close their business. Such cancellations (as well as the closure of schools) had a significant impact on the ability of publishers to bring new works to the public. I, for instance, had to postpone the publication of my new novel, *Madagali* because of the pandemic. The cancellations also reduced opportunities for writers to perform at paid speaking events.

In response to the situation, some writers offered online readings and performances using various social media tools. Services and platforms such as Zoom, Google Meet, WhatsApp, and others were and continue to be widely used by writers and artists.

Some booksellers adapted by providing free shipping and other incentives to encourage book buying. While some bookshops continued to offer book deliveries, some de-prioritised book shipments in favour of other shipments.

Many publishers also relaxed restrictions on the digital distribution of their in-copyright works. Some notable academic publishers made thousands of books, articles, and other materials available for free download in 2020.

Libraries and Archives
Libraries and archives faced different situations: some maintained a full service with restrictions, others provided minimal services and some opted for complete closure. Many public libraries cancelled programs altogether, but some libraries imposed a wait period before handling returned books, while others said that clients were not to return borrowed books until things returned to normal.

Some libraries were also pressed into service for the COVID-19 response. For example, in Kenya, the National Library Service's computer lab became the Taita Taveta County data-entry and analysis centre for COVID-19 tests.

Libraries of different sizes and purposes around the world worked to provide access to collections and services remotely. For example, the Ghana Library Authority provided childhood literacy classes via Facebook while the National library of Israel announced it would provide free audiobooks. In Namibia, the Namibia Library and Archives Service reported that local libraries left their public wifi running overnight to provide online access to the local communities.

The restart of library services was carried out in a progressive manner, with additional methods employed to mitigate risks. These included limiting the number of simultaneous patrons, the concentration of patrons within buildings and instituting new hygiene protocols for staff and patrons.

Performing Arts and Book Festivals
Due to physical distancing requirements, many performing arts venues and schools were closed, curtailing rehearsals and public performances. Many popular book festivals in Africa such as the International Book Festival and the Ake Book Festival both in Nigeria as well as the Pa Gya literary festival in Accra, Ghana took place as virtual festivals.

THE WAY FORWARD
Financial Empowerment For Writers
Many writers face the challenge of earning a living off writing, leading to the common financial difficulties for writers who have no other profession to rely on. Having taken notice of the very small percentage of African writers who make a living from their writing careers, the Pan African Writers Association (PAWA) recently commenced an Empowerment Project for African Female Writers. The project will provide some levels of financial support for interested writers when fully operational, and will assist the writers in augmenting their incomes from writing.

Writers should also consider other revenue streams such as book sales, appearance fees, coaching other writers, writing book reviews and ghost writing to complement their royalties.

Since the advent of the global crisis, many countries have put in place palliatives for many sectors of the economy. There is an urgent need for artists to be included in such schemes.

Online Publishing

Digitalization has led to profound changes in the market for authors' works, a situation that significantly impacts their earnings. The US Authors Guild reported the growing dominance of Amazon along with lower royalties and advances for midlist books (which publishers typically blame on losses they are forced to pass on). This includes the extremely low royalties paid on sales that are deeply discounted and low net royalties of 25% on ebooks. The rise in online publishing has also encouraged a surge in self-published authors. Amazon has become one of the chief beneficiaries for the self-publishing boom, offering one of the main platforms where independent authors can sell their titles and access print-on-demand services. In many countries, Amazon is now central to both independent and traditional publishing businesses.

Virtual Meetings and Arts Events

As pointed out above, online literary activities became the vogue in beating the physical distancing that was brought about by the global pandemic. Although the practice is not as conducive as physical meetings, it has proven to be cheaper and quite appropriate for many literary activities. In view of the uncertainty in the duration of the pandemic, the practice may remain with us for a long time.

Social Media

Social media has become increasingly prevalent in the lives of authors and is viewed as particularly important for marketing purposes. Participation in social networks is now seen as crucial for authors wanting to make useful contacts and develop opportunities. A large number of authors now use social networks to promote their books, events and readings. They also use it to communicate with readers and other writers.

Improved Relationships with Publishers
There is the need for a better relationship between writers and publishers especially in Africa where many writers are paid next to nothing by their publishers in the form of royalties. For example, according to Francis Gbormittah, the President of the Ghana Writers Association (GAW), it can be difficult for authors in Ghana to receive fair treatment for their work. As he put it, "Many authors report fraudulent publishing houses buying the rights to their works and avoiding paying any royalties, sometimes even dissolving their companies to avoid scrutiny. Authors also receive next to no remuneration for the widespread copying of their work in copy-shops, a practice that undermines the market for legitimate sales of their works." Given that neither publishing nor copying are well policed or regulated, and with print piracy prevalent, Gbormittah believes that digital publishing could offer a better regulated alternative.

Legislations and Policies
While the boom in online services is good, the development needs strong copyright laws that will ensure adequate and timely remunerations for authors. When legislators consider changes to copyright frameworks, it is important that they

understand the difficulties authors routinely face in making a professional living, both in developed nations and in developing countries where the challenges can be even more significant. No copyright exception should disregard fair payment to authors for the use of their work.

Also important are legislations for endowments for artists. While many developed countries have provisions for endowments for their artists, the same is lacking in many developing countries and should not be so.

Improvement in the Reading Culture
The previously poor reading culture in many African countries may be worsened by the poverty that is likely to increase with the COVID-19 pandemic. Any increase in the levels of illiteracy, costs of book production, and the attendant distraction from social media, television and the internet will affect the ability of many African authors to make a living in their country of origin.

It is therefore very important for this problem to be tackled if we want our writers to make a decent living from their writing.

Financing for Literary Arts
With the widespread economic downturn brought about by the global pandemic, financing for the literary arts by donors, advertisers and government agencies may also experience a decline. Already, some donors have been sending signals of the impending reduction in financial support. In view of this, it

will be advisable for literary arts organizations to start reviewing their budgets in order to accommodate the likelihood of a reduction in their finances.

Collaborations

In the face of impending dwindling finances for literary activities, it will be a good idea for literary organizations to collaborate in executing their various projects. The organizations can also use the joint effort to pull resources together to achieve more. The Pan-African Writers Association (PAWA) is already collaborating with some arts organizations and is willing to do more.

Dr Wale Okediran is Secretary General of the Pan African Writers Association (PAWA). He is a Medical Doctor and a writer. He holds a diploma in Writing from the London School of Writing and has published 15 novels – 11 adult novels and 4 children's books, and 5 Biographies of some notable Nigerians. Apart from being on the reading list of some Nigerian and foreign Universities, some of Wale's books, *The Boys At The Border, The Rescue of Uncle Babs, Strange Encounters, The Weaving Looms* and *Tenants of the House* have won local and international literary prizes and recognitions which include: the Commonwealth Literature Prize, ANA/MATATU Prize for Children's Literature, the NLNG Literature Prize and the Wole Soyinka Prize for African Literature. His book, *Tenants of the House* was recently adapted into a motion picture directed by Kunle Afolayan.

Wale was the national president of the Association of Nigerian Authors from 2005 to 2009 and was once a Member of the House of Representatives for Abuja, Nigeria. He was once a hockey player for the Ife University Medical School and Oyo State, Nigeria. He is married with children and grandchildren, and enjoys reading, walking, travelling and writing.

References:

"Creating a Living: Challenges for authors' incomes." https://www.internationalauthors.org/wp-content/uploads/2020/09/Creating_A_Living_Booklet-1.pdf

Impact of the COVID-19 pandemic on the arts and cultural heritage https://en.wikipedia.org/wiki/Impact_of_the_COVID-19_pandemic_on_the_arts_and_cultural_heritage#cite_note-217

Namibia's Regional Libraries Final Report of the Regional Study and Resource Center (RSRC) Activity Evaluation https://digital.lib.washington.edu/researchworks/bitstream/handle/1773/46228/Namibia_LibraryEvaluation_FinalReport.pdf?sequence=1&isAllowed=y

You can't keep a good public library (locked) down https://www.eifl.net/news/you-cant-keep-good-public-library-locked-down

COVID-19 and the Global Library Field https://www.ifla.org/covid-19-and-libraries

COVID DEMOCRACY

Teddy Totimeh

My father was an orderly man. He set standards that I have tried to meet all my life. The folded stacks of his clothes always intimidated me with their manicured lines. They seemed to have a presence of their own, populating his wardrobe like stationary soldiers on a parade ground. Sometimes my children breeze into my bedroom, rifling through my clothes in search of all the things that children look for… and I wish I had such folded rows to intimidate them with.

I wonder what he would have thought about the times we live in. I wonder what solutions he would have proffered for these uncertain times. These times have been a perfect storm for increasing social entropy. The order that ensures that true social development is protected, is threatened on multiple fronts, and COVID seems to be the overarching master disruptor. It has challenged the fabric of our societal order, in every way. It has changed the way we live. It has threatened our very mindset of the future, as a people.

Many times, I have not seen the adherence to protocol that should keep this disease at bay. Sometimes, I have not seen the protocol at all. We have evolved as a society to fight this scourge with some of the best weapons we have. But there have been some black holes in unexpected places.

I registered as a voter at a center near my home on the very last day of the exercise. There was no queue. There was one medical person directing us to wash our hands to start the process. She was not wearing a mask. I had to prompt her. I washed my hands, and was directed to the unsanitized seat, minimally spaced from the next. Then I sat next to the lady taking down my living details. I reminded her to cover her nose. She did not like that. She gave me a thumbprint pad. I could see the numerous previous prints. I could see COVID all over the pad. She could not. She was already tired. It had been a long day.

I had no choice but to add my fingerprint, and whatever organisms the handwashing had left to the building reservoir on the pad. Then I moved to the next unsanitized seat, and I had to remind the guy behind the biometric machine to put on his mask. I could see his droplets just flying everywhere, as he joked incessantly with the various observers. He had actually previously told his colleagues that no one was going to convince him to put his mask on. So there was a lot of snickering when this lone voice from the queue firmly prevailed on him to put on his mask. He did. He sanitized the print machine before I put my fingers on it. But the last step was the doctor's nightmare.

The indelible ink was in a small container with a neck specially molded to accommodate one little finger at a time. The damp ink-soaked pad was at the bottom, with small animals from many people, many days before, multiplying slowly. A dark soup of swimming microorganisms on the fingertip of every one who left the centre. The election officer almost threw a fit when I grabbed a tissue and some alcohol and sanitized my finger tip as soon as I took it out of that fester pot. She insisted the ink was going to rub off, I reminded her that it was indelible. I could not help but think of all the people who had walked away with millions of microorganisms on their fingerprints, and the indelible mark of democracy.

Maybe we have been spared the worst of this pandemic. It seems so. It seems like we have done everything we can to provoke this virus that has wreaked havoc in other places, and we have continued to cruise. I don't know whether it is a matter of timing, or it is just that we are built to be spared the brunt. Brazil and India felt protected when this virus was razing Europe. COVID has left catastrophe in these two countries since it traversed their borders.

We must keep our shape, maintain whatever order we have and keep the formation on the battle ground.

The battle is not over yet.

ON UNITY

Teddy Totimeh

I was driving behind this guy when he lurched into my lane. I had to slam hard on my brakes, just to save my day. He was completely oblivious of what had happened, as I passed him. He was focused on the road ahead, and seemed to be nodding to some music only he could hear in his air-conditioned car. Moments like these make me miss driving in more predictable environments with a communal commitment to rules and guidelines. Sometimes this dedication is really admirable to see. In a country not my own, I drove a manual car on the opposite side, with the steering wheel in the wrong place, gear lever turned all upside down… and I still had more peace of mind than I have driving in Accra on a quiet day.

There must be a requirement to sign a certain social contract that binds us to forge a certain oneness for mutual progress. Maybe it's something about urbanization. There is a certain commitment to social well-being that I have seen in the few villages I have been privileged to live in that gets lost in the city. Sometimes it seems as if in outsourcing essential services to government agencies, we have also outsourced some of our humanity. Some of that innate capacity to keep an eye out for the other person disappears. So we live in small bubbles. The true actualisation of life in the urban jungle is how secure the bubble gets to be. And in the rat race that survival has become, the walls of the bubble are reinforced for the independent survival of each inhabitant. Security is individually guarded with high walls and barbed wire. Water supply secured with a big black tank, a pump and a borehole. The waste disposal covered with a deep manhole, lodged somewhere in the hidden sector of the compound. Sometimes the electrical supply is covered with the silent generator and the shiny solar panels. And the SUVs parked in the compound have the horrible roads covered.

Enter COVID-19, the game changer. This disease has wrecked economies, ravaged health systems. It is here, and the transformations are clear. We seemed to have had some control initially, but not now. Its tentacles have reached across social lines, party lines, financial barriers. And the more impenetrable the bubbles remain, the faster it will spread. This virus preys on social irresponsibility. The only way to win any battles against it would be for one to consider the other as a fellow bubble inhabitant. The only way to defeat this disease would be to reverse all the work that has been done to build these independent bubble castles. There is a certain social responsibility needed to fight this disease. We do not have it… yet. The walls of our bubbles are too solid to transmit the care that social responsibility thrives on. There are just too many manholes, and generators, and SUVS, and boreholes for real communal initiative to thrive.

Any failure in our battle against this disease is berthed in the absence of oneness. The voice of political leadership has been split by our partisanship. The efforts at giving help to those who need it most during times of mandatory masking and physical distancing are torn apart by party loyalties. The medical voice, the scientific message, the voice on the streets split. What's one to do when authority one day locks down and another day releases a market place unto the streets?

And so, at a time like this when the disease has taken hold in the community, when people should be laying low, so that the spread slows down, we are moving people back to school. We are mixing them up at voter registration centers, and people are ignorant enough to think that face shields can replace face masks. Slowly the number of those who do not believe that COVID exists is growing. Fighting this disease is an information battle and we have lost it. The viral tentacles continue to tighten their grip on our social fabric. The storm has broken. We have lost some battles but we have not lost the war. We have learnt quite a bit, and we still have a little time on our side to make the right decisions.

But the battle can only be won if we are one.

Teddy Totimeh is a neurosurgeon working with the University of Ghana Medical Centre. He has published poetry, social commentary and short stories. He was the pioneer producer of the Open Air Theatre, a popular literary art radio programme which continues to run on Radio Univers. He has also been a co-presenter of the Writers' Project on Citi FM. He is married to Maamle, and they have 3 lovely children. Teddy loves scrabble and music.

ABOUT THE EDITORS

Mamle Kabu, a writer of Ghanaian and German parentage, was born in Ghana, and raised in Ghana and the UK. She attended the University Primary School at Legon and had part of her secondary education in Achimota school. She holds a BA and MA in Modern Languages and an MPhil in Latin American Studies from the University of Cambridge, as well as an MA in Creative Writing from the University of Lancaster, UK. Her short stories have been published in various anthologies and journals. In 2009, she was shortlisted for the Caine Prize for African Writing for her story *The End of Skill*. Mamle is a director of the Writers Project of Ghana (WPG).

Chuma Nwokolo is a Nigerian lawyer and writer. Called to the bar in 1984, he has written a dozen books, including the novels *Diaries of a Dead African* and *The Extinction of Menai*. His short story collections include *How to Spell Naija in 100 Short Stories (Vols 1 & 2)* and *The Ghost of Sani Abacha*. He is the convener of the Good Governance Campaign, bribecode.org.

Nancy Henaku is currently co-director of the writing center at Ashesi University. She earned her doctoral degree in Rhetoric, Theory and Culture (RTC) from Michigan Technological University, USA. Her research examines the cultures and politics of African rhetorical traditions with particular emphasis on transnational flows and influences.

Edzordzi Agbozo is a poet, writer, editor, and academic. His poems appeared in Prairie Schooner, North Dakota Quarterly, Dunes Review, Oakland Review, Drift, Kalahari Review, U.P. Reader, and anthologized in *According to Sources: An Anthology of Poetry*, *Intercontinental Anthology of Poetry on Universal Peace*, and elsewhere. He currently teaches at Michigan Technological University, USA.

Martin Egblewogbe is author of the collections of short stories *The Waiting* and *Mr Happy and the Hammer of God and other short stories*. Several of his other stories have appeared in various anthologies. He is a senior lecturer in Physics at the University of Ghana, and a director of the Writers Project of Ghana.